Stickers

GRADE 4-5

Kumon Summer Review & Prep

After finishing each day's math and reading exercises, paste a sticker for each subject on the calendar. When you have completed all of the pages, paste the biggest sticker under "Goal!" Congratulations on your achievement!

CONGRATULATIONS

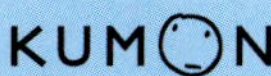

GRADE 4-5 45 Days of Kumon

KUMON

After finishing each day's math and reading exercises, paste a sticker in the appropriate place below. Make a note of any questions or difficulties in the blank space provided so you can review them later. You can also note what you learned or that day's accomplishment.

To parents: If your child seems to be having difficulty pasting the stickers or writing the date or notes, you can offer to help. When he or she has completed all of the pages, offer lots of praise and paste the biggest sticker under "Goal!" Finally, please fill out your child's name and sign your name along the bottom.

How to use this sheet

Keep your skills sharp all summer long!

- Paste a sticker here for completing a math exercise.
- Paste a sticker here for completing a reading exercise.
- Write about your questions, difficulties or accomplishments here.

Day	Date	Math	Reading	Notes
1	/ /			• •
2	/ /			• •
3	/ /			• •
4	/ /			• •
5	/ /			• •
6	/ /			• •
7	/ /			• •
8	/ /			• •
9	/ /			• •
10	/ /			• •
11	/ /			• •
12	/ /			• •
13	/ /			• •
14	/ /			• •
15	/ /			• •
16	/ /			• •
17	/ /			• •
18	/ /			• •
19	/ /			• •
20	/ /			• •
21	/ /			• •
22	/ /			• •
23	/ /			• •
24	/ /			• •
25	/ /			• •
26	/ /			• •
27	/ /			• •
28	/ /			• •
29	/ /			• •
30	/ /			• •
31	/ /			• •
32	/ /			• •
33	/ /			• •
34	/ /			• •
35	/ /			• •
36	/ /			• •
37	/ /			• •
38	/ /			• •
39	/ /			• •
40	/ /			• •
41	/ /			• •
42	/ /			• •
43	/ /			• •
44	/ /			• •
45	/ /			• •

Goal!

______________ is hereby congratulated on completing Summer Review & Prep 4-5. Presented on ________, 20______ PARENT OR GUARDIAN ______________

KUMON

GRADE 4-5

Kumon Summer Reading List

This list is designed to include a variety of genres, writing styles, cultures and authors. Please use this list as a guide for reading during the summer.

How to use this list

- Write the date you start reading the book.
- Write the date you finish reading the book.
- Write your opinions and/or questions about the book.
- Aim to read all ten books during the summer.

TO PARENTS: The Kumon Summer Reading List is designed to encourage children to develop independent reading skills. Children who acquire strong reading skills often enjoy a more successful and enriching educational experience. This list offers suggestions for quality books for readers between 4th and 5th grade. Please encourage your child to visit the library for more books.

1 The Phantom Tollbooth

By Norton Juster
Illustrated by Jules Feifer
Random House

Milo, a bored ten-year-old, finds a large toy tollbooth sitting in his room. With his "watchdog" Tock, Milo drives through it and begins a memorable journey.

Start / / Finish / /

2 The Girl Who Loved Wild Horses

By Paul Goble
Simon & Schuster

For most people, being swept away in a horse stampede during a raging thunderstorm would be a terrifying disaster. For one young Native American girl, it is a blessing.

Start / / Finish / /

3 The Big Wave

By Pearl S. Buck
HarperCollins

Kino, a Japanese boy who lives on a farm, must face life after escaping the tidal wave destruction of his family and village.

Start / / Finish / /

4 Help! I'm a Prisoner in the Library!

By Eth Clifford
HarperCollins

Two girls spend an adventurous night trapped inside the public library during a terrible blizzard.

Start / / Finish / /

5 Henry Reed, Inc.

By Keith Robertson
Illustrated by Robert McCloskey
Penguin

Thirteen-year-old Henry is an entrepreneur and establishes a business with his neighbor Midge. Together they turn a profit, which is often hazardous to the adults involved.

Start / / Finish / /

SUMMER REVIEW & PREP

6 Mrs. Frisby and the Rats of NIMH

By Robert C. O'Brien
Illustrated by Zena Bernstein
Simon & Schuster

Mrs. Frisby, a mouse, must move her family or face almost certain death. Fortunately, she meets the rats of NIMH, an extraordinary breed, who have a brilliant solution.

Start / / Finish / /

7 The Invention of Hugo Cabret

By Brian Selznick
Scholastic Press

Twelve-year-old Hugo lives in a train station where he keeps his life as an orphan, clock keeper and thief a secret. But suddenly the toy booth owner puts his world in jeopardy.

Start / / Finish / /

8 My Side of the Mountain

By Jean Craighead George
Penguin

In this enthralling story, a boy builds a treehouse in the mountains and learns to live entirely by his wits.

Start / / Finish / /

9 It's Like This, Cat

By Emily Cheney Neville
Illustrated by Emil Weiss
HarperCollins

Dave and his father argue – a lot. By meeting some special people, Dave comes to understand his family a little better.

Start / / Finish / /

10 Tuck Everlasting

By Natalie Babbitt
Farrar, Straus, and Giroux

For the Tuck family, the fountain of youth and living forever is a reality, but their reaction to their fate is surprising.

Start / / Finish / /

Multiplication

Date / /

Name

Level ★

Score /100

Math DAY 1

1 Multiply. 5 points per question

(1) 13×2

(2) 34×2

(3) 23×3

(4) 43×3

(5) 32×4

(6) 43×4

(7) 24×5

(8) 37×5

(9) 27×6

(10) 48×6

(11) 31×7

(12) 53×7

(13) 25×8

(14) 39×8

(15) 16×9

(16) 57×9

(17) 60×4

(18) 73×2

(19) 36×3

(20) 84×5

Reading DAY 1

Vocabulary

Syllables

Date / / Name

Level ★ Score /1

1 Read each word aloud. Then divide the word into syllables. 10 points per ques

(1) airplane air/plane

(2) parachute ______

(3) scrapbook ______

(4) automobile ______

(5) highway ______

(6) computer ______

(7) basketball ______

(8) spectators ______

2 Write the words with the same amount of syllables in each group below. 20 points for corr

alligator	propeller	hollow	overboard	pelican
motorcycle	dictionary	badger	hurdle	

(a) 2 syllables (b) 3 syllables (c) 4 syllables

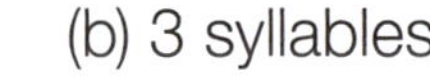

dictionary

Don't forget! A **syllable** is a unit of sound that makes up a word.

Math DAY 2

1 Multiply. 5 points per question

(1) 130×4

(2) 273×2

(3) 408×3

(4) 318×3

(5) 116×4

(6) 347×4

(7) 227×5

(8) 547×5

(9) 409×6

(10) 647×6

(11) 503×7

(12) 381×7

(13) 308×8

(14) 459×8

(15) 207×9

(16) 728×9

(17) 274×6

(18) 686×7

(19) 778×8

(20) 889×9

Reading DAY 2

Vocabulary
Adverbs

Date / /　Name

Level ★　Score /100

① Complete the table below according to the example. 50 points for completion

adjective	adverb
immediate	immediately
deliberate	
normal	
polite	
rapid	
playful	
swift	

adjective	adverb
lazy	lazily
sleepy	sleepily
merry	
helpful	
generous	
light	
dainty	daintily

② Read the passage. Then answer the questions below using only adverbs from the passage. 10 points per question

An old woman with a large bag boarded a bus that rapidly drove away. Immediately, a young man generously gave his seat to her. Normally, most people would swiftly take the seat and politely thank the man for being so helpful. Instead, the woman daintily laid her bag on the seat and remained standing. Was the woman deliberately being rude? No, she merrily explained that inside the bag was a litter of sleepy kittens. She was carefully taking them to a new home.

(1) How did the bus drive?

The bus drove ____________.

(2) When did the young man give up his seat?

The young man gave up his seat ______________.

(3) How would people normally react to the young man's offer?

Normally, most people would ___________ thank the man.

(4) How did the woman lay her bag down?

The woman laid her bag down ___________.

(5) How was the woman taking the kittens to a new home?

The woman was ____________ taking the kittens to a new home.

Don't forget! An **adverb** is a word that describes a verb. Adverbs usually have "ly" as a suffix.

Multiplication

Level ★★

Date / /

Name

Score /100

Math DAY 3

 Multiply.

5 points per question

(1) $\begin{array}{r} 32 \\ \times 12 \\ \hline \end{array}$

(2) $\begin{array}{r} 42 \\ \times 23 \\ \hline \end{array}$

(3) $\begin{array}{r} 43 \\ \times 34 \\ \hline \end{array}$

(4) $\begin{array}{r} 54 \\ \times 37 \\ \hline \end{array}$

(5) $\begin{array}{r} 34 \\ \times 45 \\ \hline \end{array}$

(6) $\begin{array}{r} 46 \\ \times 42 \\ \hline \end{array}$

(7) $\begin{array}{r} 23 \\ \times 52 \\ \hline \end{array}$

(8) $\begin{array}{r} 38 \\ \times 55 \\ \hline \end{array}$

(9) $\begin{array}{r} 47 \\ \times 60 \\ \hline \end{array}$

(10) $\begin{array}{r} 28 \\ \times 61 \\ \hline \end{array}$

(11) $\begin{array}{r} 32 \\ \times 74 \\ \hline \end{array}$

(12) $\begin{array}{r} 53 \\ \times 72 \\ \hline \end{array}$

(13) $\begin{array}{r} 29 \\ \times 81 \\ \hline \end{array}$

(14) $\begin{array}{r} 34 \\ \times 83 \\ \hline \end{array}$

(15) $\begin{array}{r} 26 \\ \times 93 \\ \hline \end{array}$

(16) $\begin{array}{r} 54 \\ \times 91 \\ \hline \end{array}$

(17) $\begin{array}{r} 50 \\ \times 41 \\ \hline \end{array}$

(18) $\begin{array}{r} 67 \\ \times 24 \\ \hline \end{array}$

(19) $\begin{array}{r} 35 \\ \times 38 \\ \hline \end{array}$

(20) $\begin{array}{r} 84 \\ \times 58 \\ \hline \end{array}$

Vocabulary
Silent Letter Words

Date / /

Name

Level ★

Score /100

1 Trace the words below. 55 points for completion

(1) knead
(2) wrench
(3) kneel
(4) knuckles
(5) bomb
(6) pneumonia
(7) limb
(8) cologne
(9) wreckage

2 Choose a word from the list above to complete each sentence. 5 points per question

(1) My dad always puts on __________ before he goes to work.

(2) The divers searched the __________ for lost treasure.

(3) The mechanic asked his assistant for a __________.

(4) The baker will __________ the dough before rolling it out.

(5) After I practiced on the punching bag, my __________ hurt.

(6) Her cousin went to the hospital because she had __________.

(7) The movie was a box-office __________. It got terrible reviews.

(8) The dog broke his leg, so the doctors put a cast on the __________.

(9) When we finally got to the cave, we had to__________ because the ceiling was so low.

Multiplication

Level ★★

Date / /

Name

Score /100

Math DAY 4

1 Multiply.

5 points per question

(1) 322×13

(2) 322×33

(3) 314×14

(4) 314×45

(5) 407×24

(6) 423×51

(7) 906×37

(8) 316×70

(9) 609×55

(10) 370×38

(11) 135×16

(12) 534×47

(13) 412×67

(14) 619×58

(15) 270×50

(16) 164×56

(17) 672×32

(18) 608×89

(19) 731×44

(20) 345×95

Vocabulary

Animals

Date / /

Name

Level ★

Score /10

① Complete the passage using vocabulary words defined below.

10 points per question

The sloth is an animal that lives up to its name, which means "laziness." These (1) mammals are (2)________ for being slow and sleeping up to twenty hours a day. Sloths (3)________ in the trees of the tropical forests in Central and South America. While their (4)________ arms and wooly fur make them look like monkeys, they are more closely related to armadillos and anteaters. There are two main (5)________ of sloth. Sloths with two toes hang upside-down, while sloths with three toes like to sit upright. Three-toed sloths also have an extra (6)________ in their necks so they can turn their heads almost all the way around. Both types of sloth are slow. In fact, they're so slow that (7)________ grows on their fur. Some scientists think that sloth moves slow so (8)________ won't see them. The green algae also acts as (9)________. But they're not only slow moving—a sloth can take up to a month to (10)________ one meal.

infamous	have a bad reputation
vertebrae	a section of bone or cartilage that make up the spinal column
dwell	to stay for a while; to live in a place
algae	any plant or plantlike living creature similar to seaweed
species	a category of living things; a class of things of the same kind and with the same name
digest	to break down food and absorb it in the body
predators	animals that lives by killing and eating other animals
camouflage	the hiding or disguising of something by covering it up or changing the way it looks
mammals	warm-blooded animals with verterbrae that feed their babies with window.
lengthy	very long

Multiplication

Level ★★

Score /100

Math DAY 5

Date / /

Name

1 Multiply.

5 points per question

(1) 1140×2

(2) 1273×3

(3) 2124×4

(4) 2315×5

(5) 3112×6

(6) 1307×7

(7) 1005×8

(8) 1084×9

(9) 2004×6

(10) 2107×4

(11) 132×123

(12) 115×134

(13) 122×146

(14) 213×158

(15) 201×113

(16) 230×125

(17) 216×107

(18) 204×109

(19) 270×261

(20) 163×310

Vocabulary

Science

Date / /

Name

Level ★

Score /10

① Complete the passage using vocabulary words defined below.

10 points per quest

Get a ping-pong ball, a rubber ball, and a wooden ball of the same size. Place all three in water. Ever (1)______________ why the ping-pong ball floats the best and the wooden ball is almost underwater? It's easy to see that light objects filled with air, like (2)______________ rafts, are good at floating. But solid things can float too. Why? A Greek (3)____________ named Archimedes, who was born around 287 BC, was able to explain this (4)__________________. Archimedes' first (5)__________ was that floating objects are held up by a thrust called (6)______________. His second idea was that the force needed to keep the object (7)______________ was equal to how much water the object (8) ______________. After a lot of (9)__________________, Archimedes could (10)__________ that the amount of upward force on a floating object is equal to the weight of the water it moves out of place.

ponder	think about something carefully
inflatable	able to fill with air or gas
phenomenon	a fact, feature, or event of scientific interest
scientist	a person skilled in science
theory	an idea that is the starting point for argument or investigation
experiments	tests; an operation carried out in order to discover something
afloat	carried on or as if on the water
buoyancy	the tendency to float or to rise when in a fluid
displaced	removed from an usual or proper place
prove	to show the truth by evidence

 Multiply.

5 points per question

(1) 61×8

(2) 572×7

(3) 47×5

(4) 66×8

(5) 245×4

(6) 809×7

(7) 3204×5

(8) 6552×9

(9) 104×9

(10) 753×7

(11) 69×29

(12) 105×24

(13) 246×53

(14) 93×39

(15) 741×56

(16) 230×80

(17) 87×30

(18) 618×73

(19) 50×46

(20) 208×319

Vocabulary Crossword

Level ★

Date / / Name Score /10

① Complete the crossword puzzle using the sentences below as clues. 10 points per question

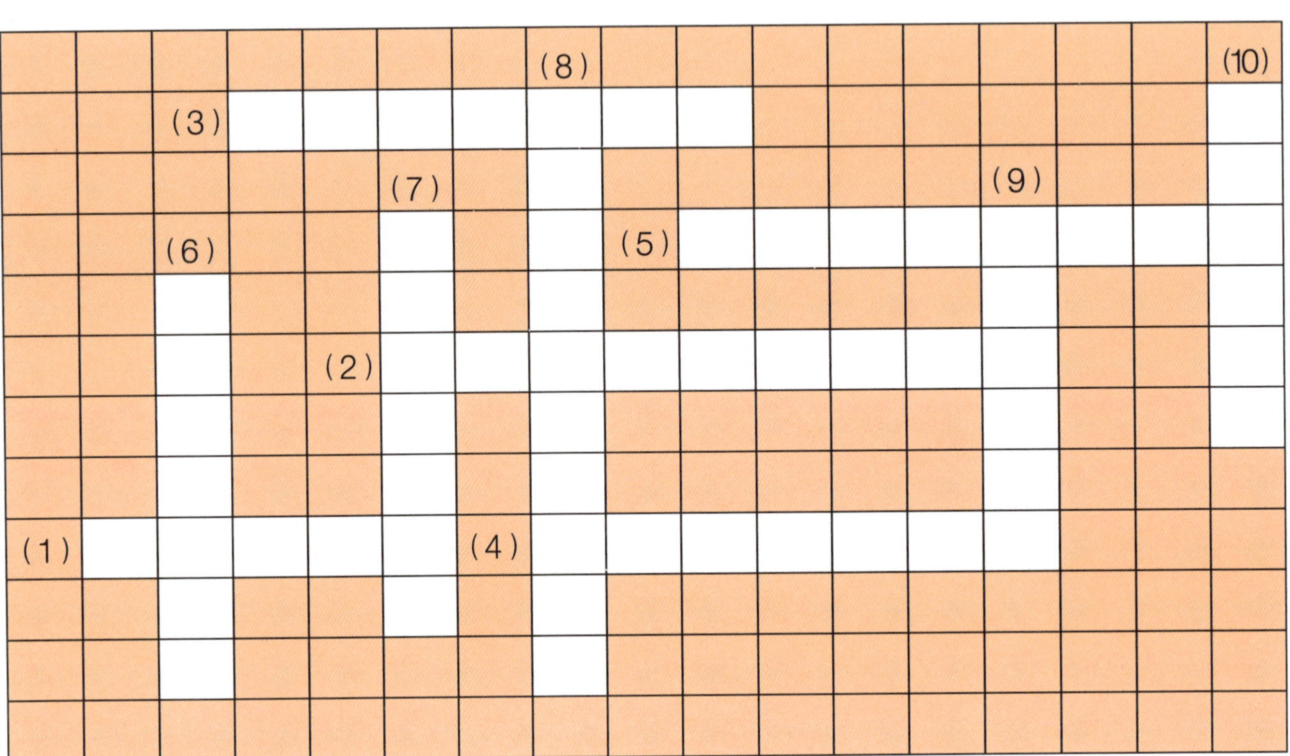

ACROSS

(1) Groups of monkeys still ________ in these forests.

(2) The stunt woman opened her ________ about 800 meters or 2600 feet from the ground.

(3) The man had sprayed on too much ______.

(4) A new ______ of frog was discovered by scientists.

(5) The man was saved from the ________ of the crashed car.

DOWN

(6) We got on the wrong __________ and drove in the wrong direction.

(7) I ________ finished my test so I rechecked my answers.

(8) The chef __________ crushed pepper over the salad.

(9) Her family _______ in church when they are praying.

(10) Our music teacher tried to explain the _______ behind harmonies.

Division

Date / /

Name

1 Divide.

4 points for completion

(1) $2\overline{)\,14}$ □

(2) $2\overline{)\,25}$ □□ R □

(3) $2\overline{)\,30}$ □□

(4) $2\overline{)\,54}$

(5) $3\overline{)\,24}$

(6) $3\overline{)\,28}$ □ R □

(7) $3\overline{)\,36}$

(8) $4\overline{)\,32}$

(9) $4\overline{)\,41}$

(10) $4\overline{)\,56}$

(11) $5\overline{)\,40}$

(12) $5\overline{)\,43}$

(13) $5\overline{)\,60}$

(14) $6\overline{)\,30}$

(15) $6\overline{)\,55}$

(16) $6\overline{)\,78}$

(17) $7\overline{)\,42}$

(18) $7\overline{)\,57}$

(19) $7\overline{)\,84}$

(20) $8\overline{)\,48}$

(21) $8\overline{)\,60}$

(22) $8\overline{)\,90}$

(23) $9\overline{)\,54}$

(24) $9\overline{)\,65}$

(25) $9\overline{)\,99}$

Reading DAY 7

Defining Words by Context

Canada

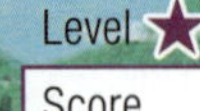

Level ★

Date / /

Name

Score /1

① Read the short passage. Then choose words from the passage to complete the definitions below. 10 points for compl

Canada is the second largest country in the world, but it only has half of one percent of the world's **population**. That means a lot of open space. Canada has lakes, rivers, mountains, **plains**, forests, and swamps. It even has the only **temperate** rain forest in the world. Canada **spans** more than half of the Northern **Hemisphere**. In the far north of Canada, you can see ice, snow, and **glaciers**.

With all this space comes many different animals—bears, mountain lions, otters and many freshwater fish. Canadians **cherish** nature and wildlife. Forty-one national parks and three marine **conservation** areas have been made to protect animals like the wolf and **lynx**. These animals need to be protected because they have been **overhunted**.

(1) ________________ large bodies of ice that move slowly

(2) ________________ to hold dear; to keep with care and affection

(3) ________________ a careful protection of something

(4) ________________ broad areas of level or rolling treeless country

(5) ________________ a large wild cat

(6) ________________ the whole number of people living in a country or region

(7) ________________ hunted too much

(8) ________________ a climate that is usually mild without very cold or hot temperatures

(9) ________________ reaches or extends across

(10) ________________ half of the earth

Division

Date / /

Name

Level ★★

Score /100

Math DAY 8

1 Divide. 4 points per question

(1) $2\overline{)224}$ □□□

(2) $2\overline{)208}$

(3) $2\overline{)150}$

(4) $3\overline{)150}$

(5) $3\overline{)315}$

(6) $3\overline{)320}$ □□□ R □

(7) $4\overline{)140}$

(8) $4\overline{)408}$

(9) $4\overline{)350}$ □□ R □

(10) $5\overline{)350}$

(11) $5\overline{)570}$

(12) $5\overline{)473}$

(13) $6\overline{)630}$

(14) $6\overline{)450}$

(15) $6\overline{)726}$

(16) $7\overline{)455}$

(17) $7\overline{)721}$

(18) $7\overline{)500}$

(19) $8\overline{)840}$

(20) $8\overline{)454}$

(21) $8\overline{)616}$

(22) $9\overline{)198}$

(23) $9\overline{)354}$

(24) $9\overline{)505}$

(25) $9\overline{)963}$

Outstanding job!

Reading DAY 8

Defining Words by Context

Making Light

Date / / Name

(1) Read the short passage. Then choose words from the passage to complete the definitions below. 10 points per question

A long time ago people learned something that would **alter** history: people learned how to **harness** fire. By striking stones together, a person could make a **spark**. Most likely, two **minerals** were used as **equipment** for starting fires. They gave off sparks when hit with something hard. The other **method** of creating fire was rubbing wooden sticks together. Just as your hands get warm when you rub them together, the **friction** of wood being rubbed together **generates** heat. **Tinder** would be put nearby to catch fire.

When a fire is lit, it creates light. The flame's color can tell you how hot the flame is and how much energy is being **released**. A bright blue flame is very hot and a dull yellow flame is cooler.

(1) ______________ a way, plan, or procedure for doing something

(2) ______________ a bright flash; a small bit of burning material

(3) ______________ tools; necessary items used for a purpose

(4) minerals natural materials usually from the ground

(5) ______________ causes; brings into existence

(6) ______________ to put to work; use

(7) tinder a material that burns easily

(8) ______________ set free

(9) ______________ the rubbing of one thing against another

(10) ______________ change; to make different in some particular

Division

Date / /

Name

Level ★★

Score /100

Math DAY 9

1 Divide.

5 points per question

(1) $21\overline{)46}$ = 2 R □
 42
 4

(2) $21\overline{)67}$ = □ R □

(3) $21\overline{)105}$ = □

(4) $31\overline{)221}$

(5) $32\overline{)235}$

(6) $43\overline{)120}$

(7) $47\overline{)300}$

(8) $56\overline{)290}$

(9) $53\overline{)350}$

(10) $64\overline{)470}$

(11) $67\overline{)600}$

(12) $71\overline{)362}$

(13) $76\overline{)532}$

(14) $82\overline{)422}$

(15) $88\overline{)528}$

(16) $91\overline{)275}$

(17) $94\overline{)658}$

(18) $74\overline{)296}$

(19) $85\overline{)455}$

(20) $96\overline{)864}$

Who, What, When, Where, Why & How

The Lion and the Mouse

Date / /

Name

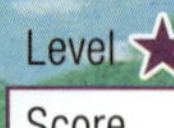

Level ★

Score

/1

① Read the passage. Then choose words from the passage to answer the questions below. 100 points for co

A mouse happened to run into the mouth of a sleeping lion, who awoke with a jolt. He pulled the frightened mouse from his mouth and was just about put him back in, when the little fellow began begging the lion to let him go. The mouse said, "If you spare my life, I shall be grateful forever and pay you back some day." The lion replied, "Haha! What good could a tiny mouse do—except to whet my appetite." But the lion thought the idea was so funny that he let the mouse go for giving him a good laugh and because the mouse was nothing more than a pre-snack snack to him.

Later that same day, the lion was running through the plains when he was caught by some hunters and bound by ropes to a tree. The mouse, hearing his roars and groans, came quickly. By gnawing the ropes, he was able to set the lion free, saying, "You laughed at me once, as if you could receive no return from me, but now, you see, it is you who have to be grateful to me." When there is a turn of events, even the most powerful can owe something to the weak.

(1) Who catches the lion?

Some __________ catch the lion.

(2) Where is the lion running when he is caught?

The lion is running through the __________.

(3) What is the lion doing when the mouse runs into his mouth?

The lion is __________ when the mouse runs into his mouth.

(4) When is the lion caught?

The lion is caught __________ that same day.

(5) Why does the mouse help the lion?

The mouse helps the lion because the lion spared the mouse's __________.

(6) How does the mouse help the lion escape?

The mouse helps the lion escape by __________ the ropes.

5 points per question

(1) 21) 275 = 1□ R □

    21
    65
    □□
     □

(2) 21) 665 = □□ R □

(3) 27) 631

(4) 31) 335

(5) 31) 639

(6) 36) 989

(7) 43) 500

(8) 44) 903

(9) 47) 982

(10) 58) 815

(11) 21) 1357 = 6□ R □

(12) 41) 2222

(13) 53) 3571

(14) 65) 4456

(15) 71) 5248

(16) 83) 2713

(17) 97) 7324

(18) 23) 4996 = □□□ R □

(19) 33) 7133

(20) 42) 8534

Reading DAY 10

Who, What, When, Where, Why & How

How to Find a Special Princess 1

Date / /　　Name

Level ★　Score /1

① Read the passage. Then choose words from the passage to answer the questions below. 100 points for cor

Once upon a time there was a prince who wanted to marry a princess, but she had to be a special princess. So he traveled east, then west, then north, and then south. There were plenty of princesses, but he could not find one that he considered special. In each case there was some little defect, which made him unsure. So he came home again in very low spirits. He thought he would be alone forever.

The night after the prince's return there was a dreadful storm; there was thunder and lightning and the rain streamed down in torrents. It was fearsome! There was a knocking heard at the palace gate, and the old king and queen went to open it.

There stood a princess outside the gate; but oh, she looked dreadful from the rain and the storm! The water was running down from her hair and her dress into the points of her shoes and out at the heels again. Her hair was a mess, whipping this way and that way from the wind. But she said she was a princess and had come to marry the prince.

(1) Who answered the door of the palace?

The ________ answered the door of the palace.

(2) What was the prince searching for?

The prince was searching for a ____________.

(3) Where did the prince travel?

The prince traveled ________, then ________, then ________, and then ________.

(4) When was the storm?

The storm was the night ________ the prince returned.

(5) Why was the prince in low spirits?

The prince was in low spirits because he thought he would be ________ forever.

(6) How did the princess look outside the gate?

The princess looked ____________.

 Divide.

10 points per question

(1)

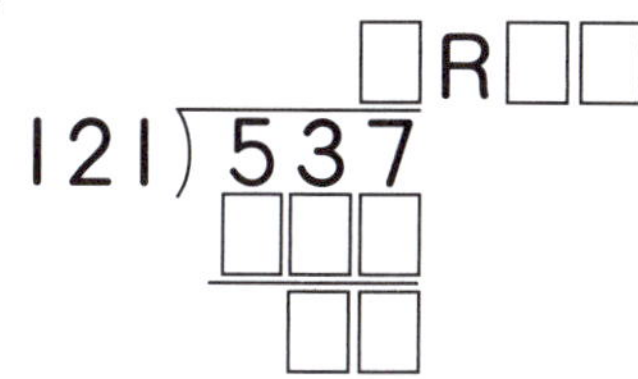

(2) 173) 888

(3) 247) 935

(4) 307) 935

(5) 324) 826

(6) 257) 8784

(7) 391) 8901

(8) 754) 9004

(9) 832) 9872

(10) 903) 9879

You're a math star!

Reading DAY 11

Who, What, When, Where, Why & How

How to Find a Special Princess 2

Date / / Name

Level ★ Score /100

① Read the passage. Then choose words from the passage to answer the questions below. 100 points for correct answers

"Well, we shall soon find out!" thought the queen. But she said nothing and snuck into the guest bedroom. She took off all the bed linens and laid a pea on the mattress. Then she put twenty more mattresses on top of the pea and twenty quilts on the top of the mattresses. And this was the bed on which the princess was to sleep.

The next morning the queen asked how the princess had slept.

"Oh, very badly!" said the princess. "I scarcely closed my eyes all night! I don't mean to be ungrateful, but I don't know what was in the bed. I laid on something so hard that my whole body is black and blue. It is worse than the storm I escaped!"

Now they saw that she was a truly special princess because she had felt the pea through the twenty mattresses and the twenty quilts. Only a true princess could be so sensitive.

So the prince asked to marry her that very moment, and the pea was put into the Royal Museum, where it still can be seen today.

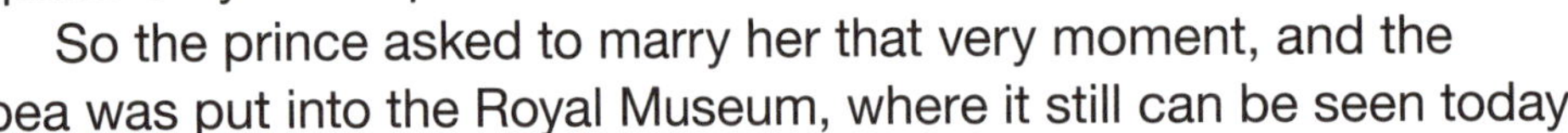

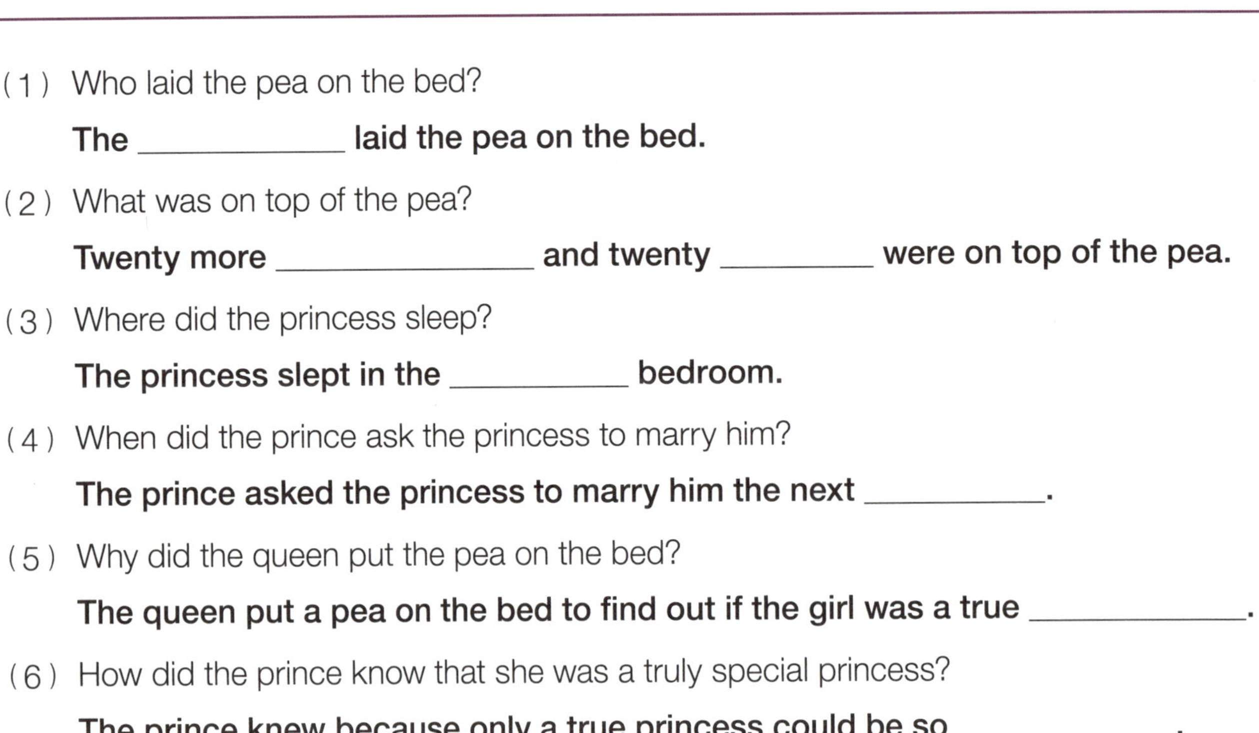

(1) Who laid the pea on the bed?

The ____________ laid the pea on the bed.

(2) What was on top of the pea?

Twenty more ______________ and twenty _________ were on top of the pea.

(3) Where did the princess sleep?

The princess slept in the __________ bedroom.

(4) When did the prince ask the princess to marry him?

The prince asked the princess to marry him the next __________.

(5) Why did the queen put the pea on the bed?

The queen put a pea on the bed to find out if the girl was a true ____________.

(6) How did the prince know that she was a truly special princess?

The prince knew because only a true princess could be so ____________.

1 Divide.

5 points per question

(1) 55) 375

(2) 7) 60

(3) 8) 5846

(4) 38) 621

(5) 52) 8061

(6) 5) 805

(7) 18) 550

(8) 63) 9036

(9) 9) 7001

(10) 42) 720

(11) 29) 1506

(12) 123) 222

(13) 251) 628

(14) 165) 5348

(15) 18) 5248

(16) 328) 1810

(17) 97) 732

(18) 257) 8993

(19) 482) 7008

(20) 142) 9500

Who, What, When, Where, Why & How

Discovering Vitamin K

Date / / Name

Score /10

1 Read the passage. Then choose words from the passage to answer the questions below. 100 points for com

Vitamins are needed by animals and plants for nutrition, growth, and life. Different vitamins have different jobs. Henrik Dam and Edward Doisy discovered vitamin K in 1934. Vitamin K is a vitamin that helps blood thicken and set. When blood sets, it forms a clot or lump and stops any bleeding.

Dam and his team discovered vitamin K by studying chicks that weren't well fed and bled easily. If the chicks had a cut it would also take a long time for the bleeding to stop. Dam believed that the chicks were missing a vitamin in their food that helped their blood clot. He found out this vitamin comes from green leaves and named it vitamin K. Dam and Doisy were able to find the vitamin in an alfalfa plant which has green leaves in a clover shape and blooms a blueish flower. They could make the chicks' blood clot better and faster by feeding them vitamin K.

In 1943, both scientists were awarded the Nobel Prize for Medicine for their research. This famous award is given each year in Stockholm, Sweden.

(1) Who discovered vitamin K?

__________ and __________ discovered vitamin K.

(2) What does vitamin K do?

Vitamin K helps blood ________ and _____.

(3) Where is the Nobel Prize given each year?

The Nobel Prize is given in __________, __________.

(4) When did Dam and Doisy discover vitamin K?

Dam and Doisy discovered vitamin K in ________.

(5) Why did the chicks bleed easily?

The chicks bled easily because they were missing __________.

(6) How could the scientists make the chicks' blood clot better and faster?

The scientists could make the chicks blood clot by ________ them vitamin K.

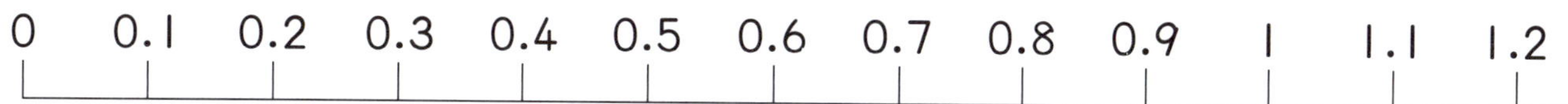

1 Write the appropriate decimal in each box. 4 points per box

(1)

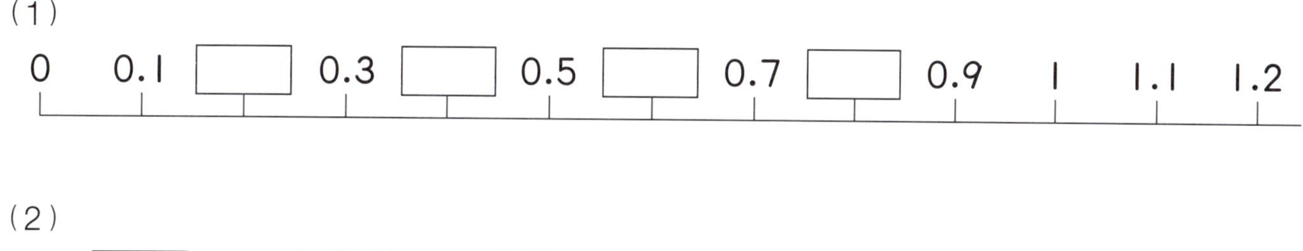

(3)

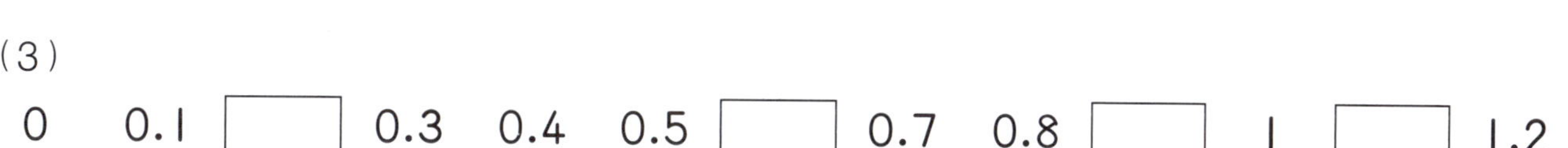

(4)

0 0.2 0.3 0.4 0.6 0.7 0.9 1.1 1.2

(5)

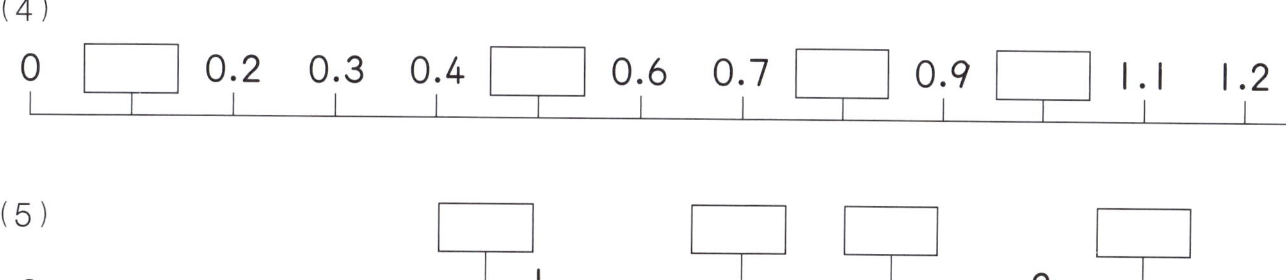

(6)

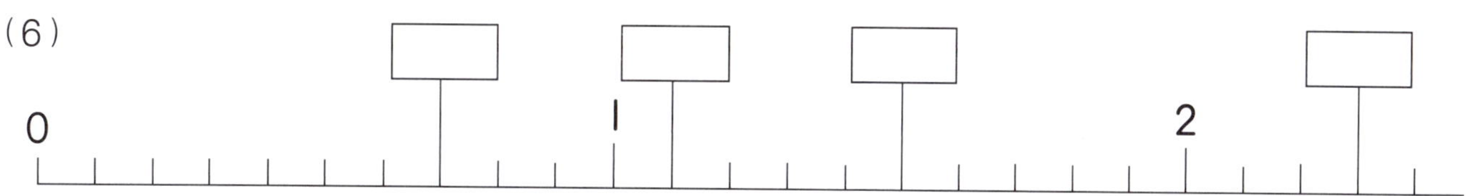

True or False

Peacekeeping

Date / /

Name

Level ★

Score /10

① Read the passage. Then read the sentences below. Circle the "T" if the sentence is true. Circle the "F" if the sentence is false. 10 points per question

After World War II, many nations decided to form a group to assure people's freedom and to work towards peace around the world. On October 24, 1945, this group was formed and it was called the United Nations. Now that day is celebrated around the world as United Nations Day. The United Nations had many goals, but they started with four main aims: to set up and maintain international peace, to grow friendships between countries, to help countries work together to fix problems, and to convince nations to respect human rights and freedoms. Fifty-one countries joined together initially to create the United Nations. As of 2011, 193 nations are members.

The United Nations has its own peacekeeping force, which includes members of the military, police, and general public who work to build peace in countries that have conflicts. Peacekeepers have been sent to countries all over the world to protect citizens and restore peace.

(1) Before World War II, many nations formed the United Nations. T F

(2) The United Nations was formed on October 24, 1945. T F

(3) October 24th is United Nations Day. T F

(4) The United Nations started with eight main goals. T F

(5) At first, fifty-one countries made up the United Nations. T F

(6) 190 nations were members as of 2011. T F

(7) One of the United Nations' goals is to grow friendships between countries. T F

(8) The peacekeepers are members of the military, police, judges and general public. T F

(9) The peacekeeping force builds peace in countries that have conflicts. T F

(10) Peacekeepers have been sent all over the world. T F

Decimals

Addition

Date / /

Name

Level ★★

Score /100

Math DAY 14

1 Add. *4 points per question*

(1) 1 + 0.5 =

(2) 2 + 0.7 =

(3) 1 + 1.5 =

(4) 1 + 0.9 =

(5) 2 + 1.3 =

(6) 0.2 + 0.7 =

(7) 0.4 + 0.6 =

(8) 0.6 + 1.7 =

(9) 1.3 + 0.5 =

(10) 1.5 + 0.7 =

(11) 1.3 + 2 =

(12) 1.9 + 1 =

(13) 1.4 + 1.2 =

(14) 2.1 + 1.5 =

(15) 1.8 + 1.7 =

2 Add. *4 points per question*

(1) 1.3 + 2.5

(2) 2.3 + 0.4

(3) 14.5 + 1.5

(4) 3.6 + 12.1

(5) 0.8 + 11.7

(6) 8 + 12.5

(7) 2.05 + 1.6

(8) 0.68 + 2.4

(9) 6.24 + 1.75

(10) 5.52 + 14.48

True or False

Exploring Deep Space

Date / /

Name

Level ★

Score /10

① Read the passage. Then read the sentences below. Circle the "T" if the sentence is true. Circle the "F" if the sentence is false. 10 points per question

Remote-control spacecraft have been flying around space for more than forty years. These explorers are "unmanned," meaning there is no person onboard the spacecraft. These crafts travel around like a stone from a slingshot. These amazing robots have gone as far as Mercury, Venus, Mars, Jupiter, Saturn, Uranus, and Neptune to get data and pictures. They are our eyes and ears in places where people cannot go. The spacecraft use each planet's gravity to pull them in and shoot them onward. Gravity is the force that holds objects down on the surface of the earth.

Yet none of these journeys would be possible without the Deep Space Network, which is a system of antennas. Antennas are devices that send and receive signals. These signals can travel up to billions of miles or kilometers. The farther a spacecraft has to go, the larger the antenna needs to be. Some antennas can be as large as a two-story house or even larger!

(1) Remote-control spacecraft have been flying around space for more than four decades. T F

(2) Spacecraft use a planet's gravity like a slingshot to pull them in and shoot them onward. T F

(3) Remote-control spacecraft have gone as far as Neptune. T F

(4) Without the Deep Space Network, we would not be able to have so many television channels. T F

(5) Unmanned spacecraft take pictures and get data. T F

(6) The Deep Space Network is a system of antennas. T F

(7) Remote-control spacecraft always have at least one pilot on board. T F

(8) Antennas are devices that only receive signals. T F

(9) The farther a spacecraft has to go, the larger the antenna needs to be. T F

(10) Signals can travel only one million miles. T F

Decimals
Subtraction

Date / /

Name

Level ★★

Score /100

Math DAY 15

1 Subtract. 4 points per question

(1) $0.8 - 0.3 =$

(2) $0.6 - 0.2 =$

(3) $1.5 - 0.2 =$

(4) $1.9 - 0.7 =$

(5) $1.4 - 0.6 =$

(6) $2.5 - 0.9 =$

(7) $1.7 - 0.7 =$

(8) $2.8 - 2 =$

(9) $3.5 - 1.3 =$

(10) $1.8 - 1 =$

(11) $2.1 - 0.3 =$

(12) $2.8 - 0.9 =$

(13) $3.5 - 1.7 =$

(14) $2.3 - 1.5 =$

(15) $3.2 - 2.8 =$

2 Subtract. 4 points per question

(1) $\begin{array}{r} 2.3 \\ -\ 1.1 \\ \hline \end{array}$

(2) $\begin{array}{r} 3.8 \\ -\ 2.5 \\ \hline \end{array}$

(3) $\begin{array}{r} 14.7 \\ -\ 0.4 \\ \hline \end{array}$

(4) $\begin{array}{r} 2.6 \\ -\ 1.8 \\ \hline \end{array}$

(5) $\begin{array}{r} 3.3 \\ -\ 1.5 \\ \hline \end{array}$

(6) $\begin{array}{r} 4.2 \\ -\ 0.6 \\ \hline \end{array}$

(7) $\begin{array}{r} 12.4 \\ -\ 3.4 \\ \hline \end{array}$

(8) $\begin{array}{r} 15.3 \\ -\ 7 \\ \hline \end{array}$

(9) $\begin{array}{r} 5.86 \\ -\ 3.5 \\ \hline \end{array}$

(10) $\begin{array}{r} 4.54 \\ -\ 1.74 \\ \hline \end{array}$

Don't forget! When you subtract decimals, align the decimal points.

Cause & Effect

The Peasant and the Bear 1

Date / / Name

Score /100

① Read the passage. Then answer the questions below.

Once upon a time there was a peasant whose wife and children left him, and so he was all alone with no one to help him in his home or his fields. So he went to the bear and said, "Look here, Bear, let's plant our garden together."

And the bear asked, "But how shall we divide it afterwards?"

"How shall we divide it?" asked the peasant. "Well, you take all the tops and let me have all the roots."

"All right, we have a deal," answered the bear.

So they sowed some potatoes, and they grew beautifully. The bear worked hard and gathered all the potatoes. Then they began to divide them. The peasant said, "The tops are yours, aren't they, the bear?"

"Yes," he answered.

So the peasant cut off all the potato tops, which were only bitter leaves and gave them to the bear. Then the farmer sat down to count the delicious potatoes. The bear realized that the peasant outwitted him and he huffily went to his cave.

(1) Why was the peasant all alone? 30 points for completion

The peasant was all alone because his ________ and ____________ left him.

(2) Number the statements below in the order in which they occurred. 30 points for completion

( ) The bear asks how they will divide the food.

( ) The peasant and the bear make a deal.

( ) The peasant asks the bear to work together.

( ) They grow potatoes and harvest them.

(3) Complete the chart with words from the passage above. 40 points for completion

Cause	Effect
The peasant is alone.	He asks the bear to ________ a garden together.
They make a deal.	The peasant gets the ____________, and the bear gets the ____________.
They sow some ____________.	The bear gets bitter ____________ and the peasant gets delicious roots.

Improper Fractions

Date / /

Name

Level ★★

Score /100

Math DAY 16

1 Rewrite the improper fractions as mixed numbers or whole numbers. 4 points per question

(1) $\frac{6}{5} = 1\frac{\square}{5}$

(2) $\frac{8}{5} =$

(3) $\frac{13}{5} =$

(4) $\frac{6}{6} = \square$

(5) $\frac{11}{6} =$

(6) $\frac{5}{4} =$

(7) $\frac{9}{4} =$

(8) $\frac{7}{7} =$

(9) $\frac{10}{7} =$

(10) $\frac{13}{7} =$

(11) $\frac{16}{7} =$

(12) $\frac{13}{8} =$

(13) $\frac{19}{8} =$

(14) $\frac{10}{9} =$

(15) $\frac{16}{9} =$

2 Rewrite the mixed numbers and whole numbers as improper fractions. 4 points per question

(1) $1 = \frac{\square}{4}$

(2) $1\frac{2}{5} = \frac{\square}{5}$

(3) $1\frac{1}{4} =$

(4) $2 = \frac{\square}{5}$

(5) $2\frac{1}{5} =$

(6) $1\frac{1}{3} =$

(7) $2\frac{2}{3} =$

(8) $2 = \frac{\square}{6}$

(9) $1\frac{3}{7} =$

(10) $1\frac{3}{9} =$

Reading DAY 16

Cause & Effect

The Peasant and the Bear 2

Date / / Name

Level ★ Score /10

① Read the passage. Then answer the questions below.

The next spring the peasant again came to see the bear and said, "Look here, Bear, let's work together again, shall we?"

The bear remembered the potato disaster from the year before and answered, "Right-ho! Only this time, I'll make the deal: you can have the tops, and I'm going to have the roots!"

"Very well," said the peasant.

But this year they sowed some wheat, and when the ears grew up and ripened, you never saw such a sight. The bear worked hard and gathered all the wheat, and then they began to divide it. This time, the peasant took all the tops with the grain for baking bread and gave the bear the straw and the roots, which weren't much good for anything. The bear realized that the peasant had outwitted him again!

"Well, good-bye!" said the bear to the peasant, "I'm not going to work with you anymore, you're too crafty!" And with that he went off into the forest.

(1) Why did the bear make a different deal? 20 points

The bear made a different deal because he remembered the ____________ from the year before.

(2) Number the statements below in the order in which they occurred. 40 points for co

( ) The bear gets the straw and roots.

( ) They grow wheat together.

( ) The bear makes a new deal.

( ) The peasant asks the bear to work together again.

(3) Complete the chart with words from the passage above. 10 points per w

Cause	Effect
The bear remembers last year's potato disaster.	He makes a new ________.
They make a deal.	The peasant gets the ________, and the bear gets the ________.
They plant .	The bear gets the ________ and roots, and the peasant gets the grain.

Fractions

Addition

Date / /

Name

Level ★★

Score /100

Math DAY 17

1 Add.

5 points per question

(1) $\frac{2}{5}+\frac{1}{5}=\frac{\square}{5}$

(2) $\frac{2}{5}+\frac{2}{5}=$

(3) $\frac{3}{5}+\frac{1}{5}=$

(4) $\frac{2}{7}+\frac{1}{7}=$

(5) $\frac{3}{7}+\frac{1}{7}=$

(6) $\frac{1}{7}+\frac{4}{7}=$

(7) $\frac{2}{7}+\frac{3}{7}=$

(8) $\frac{2}{9}+\frac{2}{9}=$

(9) $\frac{1}{9}+\frac{4}{9}=$

(10) $\frac{4}{9}+\frac{3}{9}=$

(11) $\frac{1}{5}+\frac{4}{5}=\frac{\square}{5}=\square$

(12) $\frac{2}{7}+\frac{4}{7}=$

(13) $\frac{3}{7}+\frac{4}{7}=$

(14) $\frac{1}{9}+\frac{7}{9}=$

(15) $\frac{4}{9}+\frac{5}{9}=$

(16) $\frac{2}{11}+\frac{6}{11}=$

(17) $\frac{3}{11}+\frac{5}{11}=$

(18) $\frac{4}{11}+\frac{7}{11}=$

(19) $\frac{5}{11}+\frac{4}{11}=$

(20) $\frac{2}{7}+\frac{5}{7}=$

Cause & Effect

Wetlands

Date / /

Name

Level ★

Score /1

① Read the passage. Then answer the questions below.

"Wetland" is the name for any area of land that is between dry land and water, like swamps and bogs. When you think of wetlands you may think of mud, annoying mosquitoes, and stinky odors. People have destroyed many wetlands because they didn't know their value. More than half of the wetlands in the United States have been drained, filled, or used for the disposal of garbage. However, wetlands are a very important natural resource. Wetlands are similar to rain forests and coral reefs because they are home to many different animals, plants, and fish. Certain animals, like the wood stork, are endangered because of wetland destruction. Without wetlands, these animals will no longer be able to live. Wetlands also act like a sponge and soak up flooding water, rain, or melting snow, thereby protecting people and land.

Because wetlands are in danger, animals, plants, land, and people are in danger, too. Therefore, environmental groups are starting programs to save the wetlands. Some governments are also passing laws to protect these areas.

(1) Why have people destroyed many wetland areas? 20 points

People have destroyed many wetland areas because people didn't know their ________.

(2) How are wetlands similar to rain forests and coral reefs? 20 points for comp

Wetlands are similar to rain forests and coral reefs because they are ________ to many different ________, ________, and ________.

(3) Why is the wood stork endangered? 20 points for comp

The wood stork is endangered because of ________ ________.

(4) Complete the chart with words from the passage above. 10 points per wo

Cause	Effect
Wetlands soak up water.	Wetlands protect ________ and ________ from flooding.
The destruction of wetlands	Certain animals will no longer be able to ________.
Because wetlands are in ________.	Environmental groups are starting programs to save the wetlands.

Fractions

Subtraction

Date / /

Name

Level ★★

Score /100

Math DAY 18

1 Subtract. 5 points per question

(1) $\frac{2}{5} - \frac{1}{5} = \frac{\square}{5}$

(2) $\frac{4}{5} - \frac{2}{5} =$

(3) $\frac{4}{5} - \frac{1}{5} =$

(4) $\frac{2}{7} - \frac{1}{7} =$

(5) $\frac{3}{7} - \frac{1}{7} =$

(6) $\frac{4}{7} - \frac{2}{7} =$

(7) $\frac{6}{7} - \frac{2}{7} =$

(8) $\frac{4}{9} - \frac{2}{9} =$

(9) $\frac{5}{9} - \frac{1}{9} =$

(10) $\frac{7}{9} - \frac{5}{9} =$

(11) $1 - \frac{3}{5} = \frac{\square}{5}$

(12) $\frac{7}{5} - \frac{4}{5} =$

(13) $\frac{8}{7} - \frac{5}{7} =$

(14) $1 - \frac{3}{7} =$

(15) $\frac{8}{9} - \frac{5}{9} =$

(16) $\frac{10}{11} - \frac{6}{11} =$

(17) $1 - \frac{5}{8} =$

(18) $\frac{13}{11} - \frac{7}{11} =$

(19) $1 - \frac{4}{9} =$

(20) $1 - \frac{2}{11} =$

Cause & Effect

Energy

Date / /

Name

Level ★

Score /1

① Read the passage. Then answer the questions below. 25 points per ques

Most of our electricity comes from burning coal, oil, or gas, but there is a limited amount of these fuels, and one day there will be none left. Therefore, many people are looking for new ways to create electricity from resources that won't run out—in other words, a source of renewable energy.

People also want to find new types of energy because burning coal, oil, and gas pollutes the earth. Scientists are studying ways to make energy out of sunlight, wind power, and water.

The most common renewable source of electricity is hydropower. Hydropower is popular because it is not very expensive to produce. Hydropower can be created by using the water from a waterfall. Another way is by using a river and a special dam (a barrier that controls the flow of water in a river). When water from a river passes through a dam, the water turns a machine that looks like a fan. This movement creates energy that can be captured and turned into electricity. By controlling the flow of water, people can produce more or less electricity.

(1) Why is electricity made from burning coal not considered renewable energy?

Electricity made from burning coal is not considered renewable because there is a __________ amount of coal.

(2) Why are people looking for new types of energy?

People are looking for new types of energy because coal, oil, and gas __________ the earth.

(3) Why is hydropower popular?

Hydropower is popular because it is not very __________ to produce.

(4) Complete the chart with words from the passage above.

Cause Effect	Effect
Limited amounts of coal, oil, and gas	People are looking for new ways to create __________.
Water from a river goes through a hydropower dam	The water ________ a machine that looks like a fan
Controlling the flow of water	People can __________ more or less electricity.

Word Problems

Multiplication

Level ★★

Date / /

Name

Score /100

Math DAY 19

1 Read the word problem, and write the number sentence below. Then answer the question. 20 points per question

(1) A box of pencils includes 12 pencils. If John bought 7 boxes as a present, how many pencils did he buy?

Number of pencils per box		Number of boxes		Total pencils
☐	×	☐	=	☐

Ans. ____________________

(2) Robin's school has 25 classes. There are 30 people in each class. How many people are in Robin's school?

Ans. ____________________

(3) Each pack of colored pencils has 8 colored pencils in it. Your class has 28 packs. How many colored pencils does your class have?

Ans. ____________________

(4) The gardener gave each child 15 seeds to plant. If there are 27 children, how many seeds did the gardener give away?

Ans. ____________________

(5) Stickers are sold in rolls of 24. If Julie buys 11 rolls, how many stickers does she have?

Ans. ____________________

Main Idea

Halle Berry

Level ★★

Date / /

Name

Score /10

① Read the passage. Then answer the questions below.

Halle Berry is an admired public figure in American history. She was the first African-American woman to win an Academy Award for Best Actress. The Academy Awards are presented each year by the Academy of Motion Picture Arts and Sciences to recognize achievements in film.

Halle Berry was born on August 14, 1966, in Cleveland, Ohio. She was a teenage finalist in national beauty pageants and went on to work as a model. She began acting when she was twenty-three years old. She was cast in many different roles and earned a lot of praise for her work.

In 1999, Berry even starred in a film about the historic movie star Dorothy Dandridge, who was the first African American to be nominated for the Academy Award for Best Actress. When Berry won the Academy Award in 2001, she said, "This moment is so much bigger than me. This moment is for Dorothy Dandridge, Lena Horne, [and] Diahann Carroll," and she went on to dedicate the award to actresses of color.

(1) Read each title below. For which paragraph would each make a good title? Draw a line to connect each to the appropriate paragraph. 60 points for com

(a) Halle Berry's Childhood

(b) Halle Berry's Tribute to African-American Actresses

(c) Introduction to Halle Berry and the Academy Awards

(i) First paragraph

(ii) Second paragraph

(iii) Third paragraph

(2) Put a check (✓) next to the best title for the whole passage below. 40 points for com

( ) How to Break Into Acting

( ) The Biography of Halle Berry

( ) The Academy Awards

Don't forget! The **main idea** is a statement that expresses the most important information in the passage.

1 Read the word problem, and write the number sentence below. Then answer the question. 20 points per question

(1) We had 350 inches of ribbon for our group. We divided the ribbon up equally among the 7 of us. How much ribbon did each of us get?

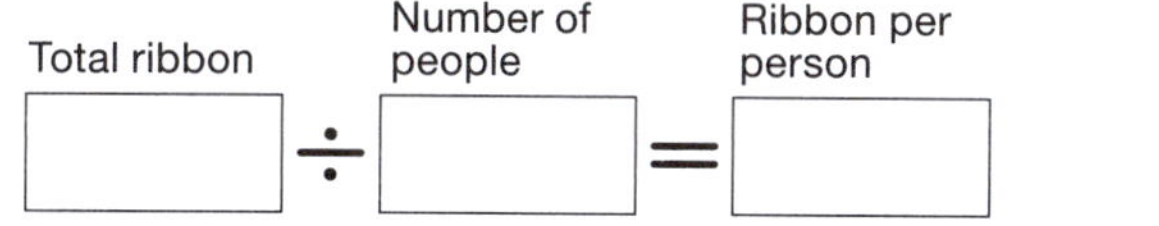

Ans. ______________________

(2) There are 204 roses, and the florist split them evenly into 12 bunches of roses. How many roses are in each bunch?

Ans. ______________________

(3) The cafeteria has 265 apples in the back. If they divide them into 8 boxes equally, how many apples are there in each box, and how many apples remain?

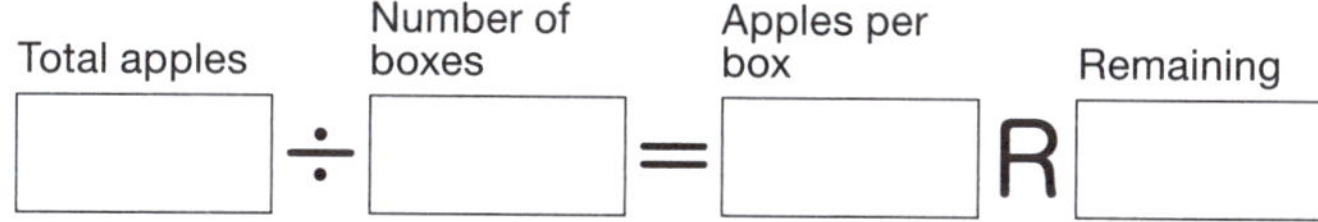

Ans. ______________________

(4) Robin has 186 lollipops at his party. If he divides them equally among the 21 people that came to his party, how many lollipops does each person get, and how many lollipops will remain?

Ans. ______________________

(5) The art teacher has 113 sheets of colored paper. If she gives 24 students an equal amount of sheets, how many sheets of colored paper does each student get?

Ans. ______________________

Reading DAY 20

Main Idea

Liquids

Level ★★

Date / /

Name

Score /10

1 Read the passage. Then answer the questions below.

A long time ago, Greeks believed that all liquids were made up of mostly water. However, scientists have discovered that all liquids are made up of particles called atoms. The smallest unit of water is a cluster of only three atoms.

Liquids can adapt to all different kinds of situations. Liquid can be thinly spread out, like when it spills across a table; or it can be tightly packed together, like when it is held in a bottle. When liquid is heated, the spaces between the particles expand and, so does the liquid. The opposite also occurs when a liquid is cooled—the particles contract and get closer together.

The tiny particles that make up a liquid are also attracted to each other and tend to keep close together. This attraction creates tension between the particles, which is why when you fill up a cup to the top, the water at the surface holds tight like the skin of a balloon. This tension also allows very light insects to walk on water. This phenomenon is called surface tension.

Liquids are also very powerful. Given enough time, liquids can wear away solid surfaces, like rocks. For example, a canyon is a deep and steep valley that has been carved out by a river. These kinds of valleys are often located where the river has a strong current that runs rapidly.

(1) Read each title below. For which paragraph would each make a good title? Draw a line to connect each title to the appropriate paragraph. **40** points for com

(a) The Discovery of Atoms — (i) First paragraph

(b) Surface Tension — (ii) Second paragraph

(c) The Power of Liquids — (iii) Third paragraph

(d) Liquid in Different Forms — (iv) Fourth paragraph

(2) Put a check (✓) next to the sentence that describes the main message of the fourth paragraph. **30** points

( ) Liquids can adapt. ( ) Liquids are powerful

( ) Canyons are made by liquid. ( ) When liquid cools, the particles contrast.

(3) What is the main idea of the whole passage? Put a check (✓) next to the correct idea below. **30** points

( ) Liquids are made up of atoms. ( ) Liquids are unchanging.

( ) Liquids have adaptable qualities. ( ) The Greeks didn't know about atoms.

1 Read the word problem, and write the number sentence below. Then answer the question. 20 points per question

(1) Mary has 208 flowers to work with today. If she puts 8 flowers into each vase, how many vases will she need?

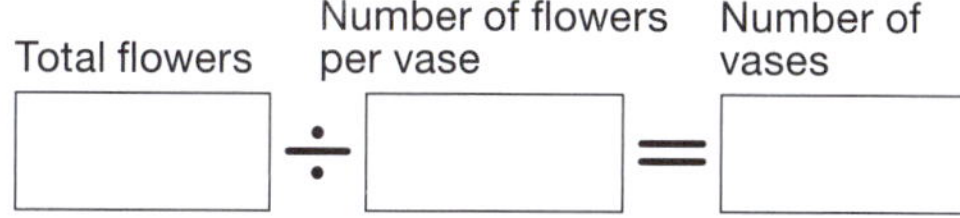

Ans. ______________________

(2) There are 194 inches of string in the art class. If the teacher cuts it and makes 16-inch segments of string, how many segments will there be, and how long will the remaining string be?

Ans. ______________________

(3) Mother bought 105 apples. If there are 6 apples in each bag at the store, how many bags did she buy, and how many apples remained?

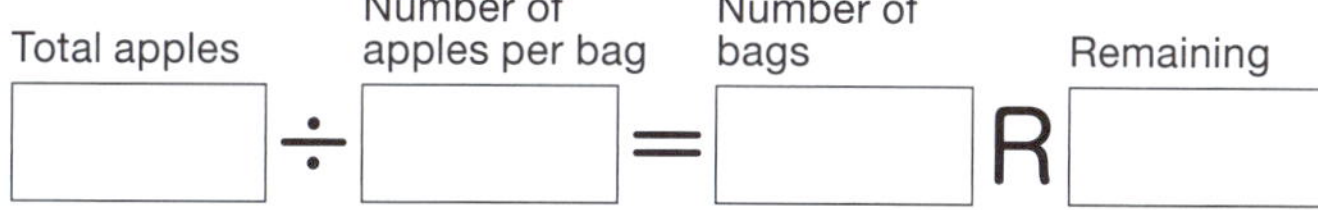

Ans. ______________________

(4) Tina has 376 inches of ribbon. If she divides it into sections that are 14 inches long, how many sections of ribbon will she have, and how long will the remaining piece of ribbon be?

Ans. ______________________

(5) Grandmother has 310 candies to send to her family. If she puts 28 candies into each box, how many boxes will she need, and how many candies will be left over?

Ans. ______________________

Main Idea

Temple Grandin

Date / /　Name

Score /1

① Read the passage. Then answer the questions below.

Temple Grandin was born on August 29, 1947, in Boston, Massachusetts. Grandin wasn't able to talk until age three. Her doctors diagnosed her as autistic. A person with autism often finds it difficult to interact and communicate with other people.

Although Grandin faced many challenges because of autism, her parents nurtured her intelligence, and she eventually went on to speak, finish high school, and study psychology in college in New Hampshire. Afterwards, she earned a master's degree and a doctorate in animal science, which was very uncommon for a woman at that time.

Because of her disability, Grandin devoted her life to learning about anxiety in people and animals and finding solutions. Grandin experienced a lot of anxiety because autistic people can be very sensitive to sound and touch. While still in high school, she designed a "squeeze machine" to help relieve her nervousness. The machine was modeled after a chute that held animals in place. Grandin's invention is now used with autistic children and adults.

However, Grandin is most well known for her innovative work with animals. She has designed humane, or more gentle, livestock facilities that eliminate pain and fear in animals. Her designs also allow workers to move animals without frightening them. She has also written several books about animal behavior.

(1) Read each title below. For which paragraph would each make a good title? Draw a line to connect each title to the appropriate paragraph. **40** points for com

(a) Grandin's First Invention　　(i) First paragraph
(b) Being Diagnosed with Autism　　(ii) Second paragraph
(c) Grandin's Legacy with Animals　　(iii) Third paragraph
(d) Grandin Succeeds at School　　(iv) Fourth paragraph

(2) What is the main idea of the whole passage? Put a check (✓) next to the correct idea below. **30** points

(　) People with autism have problems interacting with others.
(　) Temple Grandin faced many challenges.
(　) Temple Grandin was inspired by her own challenges to help anxious animals and people. **30** points

(3) What detail supports the main idea? Put a check (✓) next to the answer.

(　) Temple Grandin wasn't able to talk until age three.
(　) Temple Grandin was born on August 29, 1947.
(　) Temple Grandin studied pyschology and animal science.

You're a great reader!

Word Problems
Division

Date / /

Name

Level ★★

Score /100

Math DAY 22

1 Read the word problem, and write the number sentence below. Then answer the question. 20 points per question

(1) Kate has 54 dimes for her collection. Her younger sister has 18 dimes. How many times more dimes does Kate have than her sister?

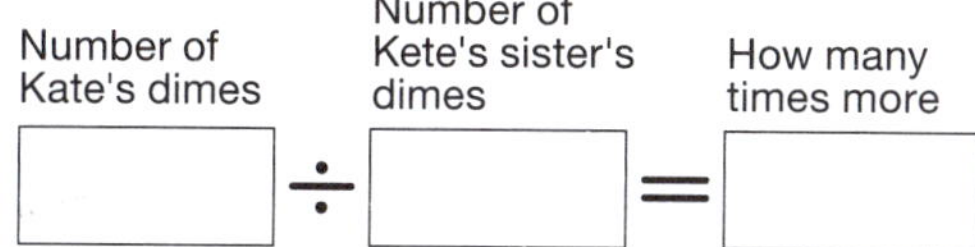

Ans. ____________________

(2) The grocer has 112 oranges in a box, and 14 oranges out front. How many times more oranges does he have in the box than he has out front?

Ans. ____________________

(3) The red ribbon in class is 36 yards long. It is 3 times longer than the blue ribbon. How long is the blue ribbon?

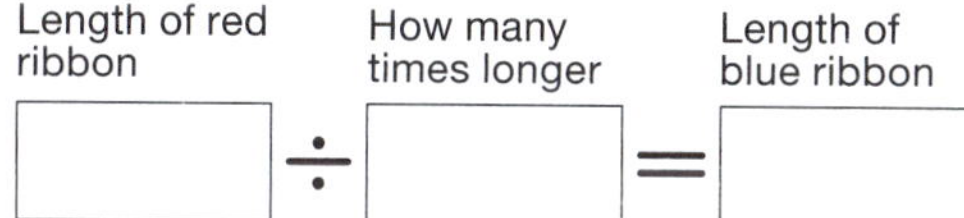

Ans. ____________________

(4) The bear at the zoo weighs 560 pounds. He weighs 7 times as much as the chimpanzee. How much does the chimpanzee weigh?

Ans. ____________________

(5) The bedroom of Smith's house is 192 square feet, and the closet is 32 square feet. How many times bigger is the bedroom than the closet?

Ans. ____________________

Main Idea

Vibrations

Date / /

Name

Level ★★

Score /10

① Read the passage. Then answer the questions below.

Did you know that glass can be shattered with only the force of the human voice? This is because of the power of vibrations, or movement back and forth. The number of vibrations that an object makes each second is called its natural frequency. Anything that can vibrate—everything from a bridge to a violin string—has its own natural frequency. Just like a swing in a playground, if an object is given a push, it will move back and forth at its natural frequency and then gradually stop. But if you continue to push a swing in the right rhythm, it can rise higher and higher. This happens when you push according to the swing's natural frequency.

The same thing happens with the shattering glass. When someone sings, his or her voice creates a sound wave that vibrates. Different notes make different sound waves and thus vibrate at different rates. If a note is sung with a rate of vibration that matches the natural frequency of the glass, the glass could shatter. When the vibrations match, the energy from the voice transfers to the glass, and the powerful vibrations destroy the glass. This transfer is called "resonance."

Luckily, there is a way to demonstrate resonance without destroying glasses. By taking a wine glass and running a wet finger quickly around the rim of the glass, a person can create a note. If the person sings the same note aloud, the glass will resonate the note and the sound will become slightly louder.

(1) Read each title below. For which paragraph would it make a good title? Draw a line to connect each title to the appropriate paragraph. 40 points per cor

(a) How a Note Can Destroy a Glass
(b) An Experiment to Show Resonance
(c) Introduction to Vibration

(i) First paragraph
(ii) Second paragraph
(iii) Third paragraph

(2) What is the main idea of the whole passage? Put a check (✓) next to the correct idea below. 30 points

( ) Science experiments are fun and informative.
( ) Vibration and resonance can be a powerful force together.
( ) Everything has its own natural rate of vibration.

(3) What detail supports the main idea? Put a check (✓) next to the answer. 30 points

( ) If you continue to push a swing at its natural frequency, it will rise.
( ) Many things—from bridges to violin strings—vibrate.
( ) Singing loudly is not good for glasses.

1 Read the word problem, and write the number sentence below. Then answer the question. 20 points per question

(1) You used 0.2 pounds of sugar in your cake, and 1.7 pounds of sugar are left over. How much sugar was there in the beginning?

Ans. ______

(2) Julian's bag weighs 2.8 pounds, and his father's bag is 1.2 pounds heavier than his. How much does his father's bag weigh?

Ans. ______

(3) Dan and Wendy were trying to throw a big rock. Dan threw it 1.3 meters. Wendy threw it 70 centimeters further. How far did Wendy throw the rock?

70 cm = 0.7 m

Ans. ______

(4) Ava's bag weighs 2.4 kilograms. Her sister's bag is 600 grams heavier. How much does her sister's bag weigh?

600 g = 0.6 kg

Ans. ______

(5) Kelly had 2.1 liters of water in her water bottle. Her big water bottle can hold 800 milliliters more. How much can her big water bottle hold?

Ans. ______

Reading DAY 23

Main Idea

Roberto Clemente

Date / /

Name

Level ★★

Score /100

① Read the passage. Then answer the questions below.

Roberto Clemente was one of the first Latin American baseball stars. He was born in a modest house in Puerto Rico on August 18, 1934. Clemente went on to become a twelve-time All Star and do important charity work in his free time.

At only fourteen years old, Clemente began playing softball on a men's team. By eighteen, he turned professional. In February of 1954, the Brooklyn Dodgers recruited Clemente but placed him in the minor leagues, where he didn't play very often. The Dodgers tried to hide his talent so other teams wouldn't want him. But it was too late—the Pittsburgh Pirates brought Clemente up to the major leagues.

Over eighteen seasons, Clemente collected impressive statistics and delighted baseball fans. No matter what kind of pitch, he could hit the ball. He had lightning speed, which made him a great base runner. He was also well known for his powerful and accurate throwing arm. Even towards the end of his career, Clemente continued to set records.

But one of the biggest challenges Clemente faced was racial prejudice. Many baseball fans, reporters, and players were rude or nasty to Clemente because he was black and Latino. However, he always defended his rights and the rights of others. Clemente said, "My greatest satisfaction comes from helping to erase the old opinion about Latin Americans and blacks."

On December 31, 1972, Clemente died in a plane crash only a few miles from where he was born. He was on his way to deliver aid to earthquake victims in Nicaragua. He was only thirty-eight, but he had become a baseball legend.

(1) Complete the main ideas for each paragraph in the chart below. 70 points for com

Paragraph	Main idea
First paragraph	Introduction to __________ __________.
Second paragraph	The start of Clemente's __________ career.
Third paragraph	Clemente ____ baseball records and delighted ______.
Fourth paragraph	Clemente faced racial ______________.
Fifth paragraph	Clemente died young but had become a baseball __________.

(2) What is the main idea of the whole passage? Put a check (✓) next to the correct idea below. 30 points

( ) Over eighteen seasons, Clemente set impressive records.

( ) Clemente helped many people and fought racial prejudice.

( ) Clemente overcame many challenges, became a baseball legend and helped people.

1 Read the word problem, and write the number sentence below. Then answer the question. 20 points per question

(1) Selena wrapped all the presents for her friends this year. If she used 1.6 yards of ribbon out of the 2.3 yards of ribbon she had, how much ribbon is left?

Ans. ________________

(2) We had 3 pounds of flour before my mother cooked me a birthday cake and used 0.3 pound of flour. How much flour do we have now?

Ans. ________________

(3) We have 2.4 liters of orange juice in the fridge. We also have apple juice, but 500 milliliters less. How much apple juice do we have in the fridge?

500 mL = 0.5 L

Ans. ________________

(4) Brad and Mark both have wizard staffs. Brad's is 2.1 meters long. If Brad's staff is 50 centimeters longer than Mark's, how long is Mark's wizard staff?

Ans. ________________

(5) My bag of pears is 0.8 kilograms heavier than your bag of pineapples. If my bag of pears weighs 2 kilograms, how much does your bag of pineapples weigh?

Ans. ________________

Reading DAY 24

Characters

The Tale of Mr. Tod

Date / /

Name

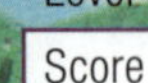

Level ★★

Score /100

① Read the excerpt from *The Tale of Mr. Tod* by Beatrix Potter. Then answer the questions below using words from the passage. 25 points per question

> I have made many books about well-behaved people. Now, for a change, I am going to make a story about two disagreeable people, called Tommy Brock and Mr. Tod. Nobody could call Mr. Tod "nice." The rabbits could not bear him; they could smell him half a mile off. He was of a wandering habit and he had foxey whiskers; they never knew where he would be next.
>
> One day he was living in a stick-house in the coppice, causing terror to the family of old Mr. Benjamin Bouncer. Next day he moved into a pollard willow near the lake, frightening the wild ducks and the water rats.
>
> In winter and early spring he might generally be found in an earth amongst the rocks at the top of Bull Banks, under Oatmeal Crag.
>
> He had half a dozen houses, but he was seldom at home.
>
> The houses were not always empty when Mr. Tod moved out; because sometimes Tommy Brock moved in; (without asking leave).
>
> Tommy Brock was a short, bristly, fat, waddling person with a grin; he grinned all over his face. He was not nice in his habits. He ate wasp nests and frogs and worms; and he waddled about by moonlight, digging things up.
>
> His clothes were very dirty; and as he slept in the daytime, he always went to bed in his boots.

(1) What type of characters will the author write a story about?

The author will write about two ______________ people.

(2) Put a check (✓) next to the words that describe Mr. Tod.

( ) nice	( ) unmoving	( ) smelly
( ) wanderer	( ) never home	( ) musical
( ) animal-friendly	( ) unpredictable	( ) funny

(3) Put a check (✓) next to the words that describe Tommy Brock.

( ) smily	( ) tall	( ) short
( ) nice	( ) dirty	( ) talented
( ) normal	( ) strange	( ) smart

(4) Despite it being daytime, what did Tommy Brock do?

Tommy Brock ______________ in the daytime.

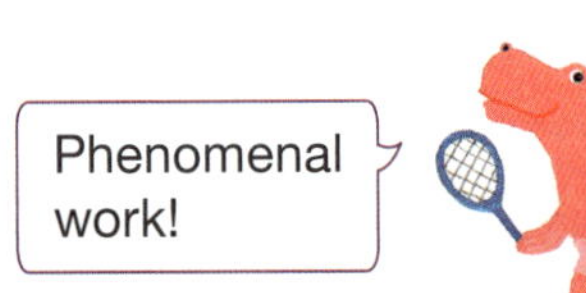
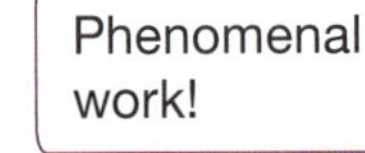

1 Read the word problem, and write the number sentence below. Then answer the question. 20 points per question

(1) At the supermarket, my mother bought some meat for $14 and some vegetables for $12. If she paid $50, how much change did she get? Using parentheses, write this down in a formula and then solve it.

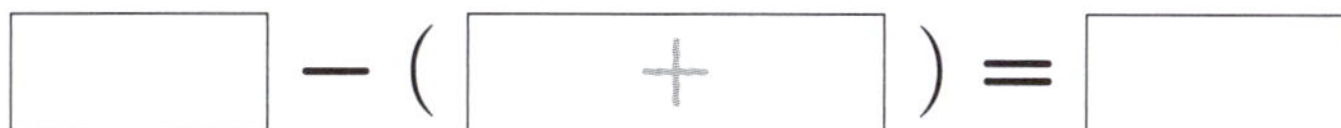

Ans. ____________________

(2) Rina's book about animals has 256 pages. She read 64 pages yesterday and 57 pages today. How many pages are left?

Ans. ____________________

(3) Jack saw a jacket that he wanted for his friend's party. He bargained with the store owner, who discounted the price $5. The jacket was originally $78, and Jack paid with a $100 bill. How much change will Jack get?

$\square - (\square - \square) = \square$

Ans. ____________________

(4) Because the dress was not popular, the shopkeeper discounted it $12. It used to cost $68. Helen bought it and paid with a $100 bill. How much change did she get?

Ans. ____________________

(5) You went shopping and bought a sandwich for $7 and a book for $12. If you paid with a $20 bill, how much change did you get?

Ans. ____________________

Don't forget! Write the problem down in a formula first and then solve it.

Characters

Clever Grethel 1

Date / /

Name

Score /1

① Read the passage. Then answer the questions below.

There was once a cook called Grethel, who wore shoes with red heels, and when she went out in them she gave herself great airs, and thought herself very fine indeed. When she came home again, she would take a drink of wine to refresh herself, and as that gave her an appetite, she would take some of the best of whatever she was cooking, until she had had enough;—"For," said she, "a cook must know how things taste."

Now it happened that one day her master said to her,—

"Grethel, I expect a guest this evening; you must make ready a pair of fowls."

"Certainly, sir, I will," answered Grethel. So she killed the fowls, cleaned them, and plucked them, and put them on the spit, and then, as evening drew near, placed them before the fire to roast. And they began to be brown, and were nearly done, but the guest had not come.

(1) Put a check (✓) next to the words that describe the Grethel. 60 points for comp

( ) angry ( ) greedy ( ) vain
( ) cook ( ) modest ( ) dirty
( ) generous ( ) stem ( ) curious

And now they began to smell so good that Grethel saying, "I must find out whether they really are all right," licked her fingers, and then cried, "Well, I never! The fowls are good; it's a sin and a shame that no one is here to eat them!"

So she ran to the window to see if her master and his guest were coming, but as she could see nobody she went back to her fowls. "Why, one of the wings is burning!" she cried presently, "I had better eat it and get it out of the way." So she cut it off and ate it up, and it tasted good, and then she thought, "I had better cut off the other too, in case the master should miss anything." And when both wings had been disposed of she went and looked for the master, but still he did not come. "Who knows," said she, "whether they are coming or not? They may have put up at an inn." And after a pause she said again, "Come, I may as well make myself happy, and first I will make sure of a good drink and then of a good meal."

(2) Why does Grethel say she must eat the first wing? 20 points

Grethel must eat the first wing because it is ______________.

(3) Why does Grethel say she should eat the whole meal? 20 points

Grethel says she should eat the whole meal because she may as well make herself __________.

1 Read the word problem, and write the number sentence below. Then answer the question. 20 points per question

(1) Alison wants to have 4 slices of cake for everyone at her party. There are 11 boys and 13 girls at her party. How many slices of cake will she need? Remember to use a formula.

Ans. ________________

(2) Jack is buying bird food for his chicken and chicks. Each day, the chicks eat 30 seeds and the chicken eats 60 seeds. If Jack wants to feed them for a week, how many seeds must he buy?

Ans. ________________

(3) Olive found a brush and comb set that she liked. The brush cost $5 and the comb cost only $3. How many sets can she buy if she has $96?

Ans. ________________

(4) Gayle and her 2 brothers gathered their money and bought a $43 racing video game and a $44 basketball video game. How much did each person pay?

Ans. ________________

(5) In the pantry, the 2 cans of beans weigh 350 grams each, and the 4 cans of beets weigh 430 grams each. How much is the total weight of the cans?

Ans. ________________

Characters

Clever Grethel 2

Date / /

Name

Level ★★

Score /1

① Read the passage. Then identify the statements as T (true) or F (false) according to the passage. 100 points for co

Just as she was in the middle of it the master came back. "Make haste, Grethel," he cried, "the guest is coming directly!" "Very well, master," she answered, "it will soon be ready." The master went to see that the table was properly laid, and, taking the great carving knife with which he meant to carve the fowls, he sharpened it upon the step.

Presently came the guest, knocking very genteelly and softly at the front door. Grethel ran and looked to see who it was, and when she caught sight of the guest she put her finger on her lip saying, "Hush! Make the best haste you can out of this, for if my master catches you, it will be bad for you; he asked you to come to supper, but he really means to cut off your ears! Just listen how he is sharpening his knife!"

The guest, hearing the noise of the sharpening, made off as fast as he could go. And Grethel ran screaming to her master. "A pretty guest you have asked to the house!" she cried.

"How so, Grethel? What do you mean?" he asked.

"What indeed!" she said. "Why, he has gone and run away with my pair of fowls that I had just dished up."

"That's a pretty sort of conduct!" said the master, feeling very sorry about the fowls. "He might at least have left me one, that I might have had something to eat." And he called out to him to stop, but the guest made as if he did not hear him. Then he ran after him, the knife still in his hand, crying out, "Only one! Only one!" meaning that the guest should let him have one of the fowls and not take both. But the guest thought he meant to have only one of his ears, and he ran so much the faster that he might get home with both of them safe.

(1) The master sharpened his knife to cut the fowl. T F

(2) Grethel told the guest the truth. T F

(3) The guest believed Grethel. T F

(4) Grethel was lying to the guest about her master. T F

(5) Grethel told her master a lie. T F

(6) Grethel found a clever way to cover up the eaten meal. T F

Word Problems

Using a Formula

Date / /

Name

Level ★★

Score /100

Math DAY 27

1 Read the word problem, and write the number sentence below. Then answer the question. 20 points per question

(1) Kate lost her dog. She made 250 fliers and gave 5 fliers each to 34 people. How many fliers did she have left over?

Ans. ______

(2) Andy saved up \$37. Today his aunt gave him \$50 and told him to divide it with his sister evenly. How much money does Andy have now?

Ans. ______

(3) It's Halloween, and your mother asked you to pick up some gumballs to give away. You bought 1 kilogram of gumballs. 2 kilograms of gumball is 820 pieces. If the store originally had 1,000 gumballs, how many pieces did the store have left after you bought 1 kilogram's worth?

Ans. ______

(4) Andy bought 3 crates of apples, and each crate held 30 apples. He also bought 1 crates of oranges. The oranges were on sale, and 5 crates held 200 oranges. How many pieces of fruit did Andy buy?

Ans. ______

(5) At Dana's party, she gave away gift bags. She divided 72 stickers into 24 bags equally. Barry took 4 bags home. How many stickers did Barry take home?

Ans. ______

Reading DAY 27

Actions & Descriptions

Black Beauty 1

Date / / Name

Level ★★ Score /100

① Read the excerpt from *Black Beauty* by Anna Sewell. Then answer the questions below.

One night, a few days after James had left, I had eaten my hay and was lying down in my straw fast asleep, when I was suddenly roused by the stable bell ringing very loud. I heard the door of John's house open, and his feet running up to the hall. He was back again in no time; he unlocked the stable door, and came in, calling out, "Wake up, Beauty! You must go well now, if ever you did;" and almost before I could think he had got the saddle on my back and the bridle on my head. He just ran round for his coat, and then took me at a quick trot up to the hall door. The squire stood there, with a lamp in his hand.

"Now, John," he said, "ride for your life—that is, for your mistress' life; there is not a moment to lose. Give this note to Dr. White; give your horse a rest at the inn, and be back as soon as you can."

John said, "Yes, sir," and was on my back in a minute.

The gardener who lived at the lodge had heard the bell ring, and was ready with the gate open, and away we went through the park, and through the village, and down the hill till we came to the toll-gate. John called very loud and thumped upon the door; the man was soon out and flung open the gate.

"Now," said John, "do keep the gate open for the doctor; here's the money," and off he went again.

(1) What was Black Beauty doing when the stable bell rang? 15 points for completion

Black Beauty was __________ down and __________ in his straw.

(2) What did John do to get Black Beauty ready to ride? 15 points for completion

John ______ the __________ on his back and the __________ on his head.

(3) What did the squire tell John he must do? 15 points

The squire told John to __________ a note to Dr. White.

(4) Describe the route that John and Black Beauty took to get to the toll-gate. 15 points for completion

John and Black Beauty went __________ the park, and the village, and __________ the hill.

(5) How did John call for the man at the toll-gate? 15 points

John called very __________ for the man.

(6) Put a check (✓) next to the words that describe the scene. 25 points for completion

( ) alarming ( ) lazy ( ) humorous
( ) relaxed ( ) important ( ) sad
( ) urgent ( ) tense ( ) boring

Don't forget! Actions are things that happen. **Descriptions** explain what something is or what something is like.

1 Read the word problem, and write the number sentence below. Then answer the question. 20 points per question

(1) The teacher brought 21 dozen colored pencils to the art class today. If she divided the pencils equally among 28 people, how many pencils did each person get?

Ans. ________________

(2) Glen bought 6 sheets that had 45 stickers on each sheet and 9 sheets that had 70 stickers on each sheet. How many stickers did he get in all?

Ans. ________________

(3) Eddie bought 5 big bags of chips for $15. His brother bought 3 small bags and paid $6. How much more expensive were Eddie's bags of chips?

Ans. ________________

(4) My piggy bank has 37 coins it. They are all pennies and nickles. If there are 5 more pennies than nickels, how many nickels do I have?

Ans. ________________

(5) Shannon has 84 stamps and her sister has 50. How many stamps does Shannon have to give her sister so that they have the same amount?

Ans. ________________

Actions & Descriptions

Black Beauty 2

Date / / Name

Level ★★ Score /100

1 Read the passage. Then answer the questions below. 20 points per question

There was before us a long piece of level road by the river side; John said to me, "Now, Beauty, do your best," and so I did; I wanted no whip nor spur, and for two miles I galloped as fast as I could lay my feet to the ground; I don't believe that my old grandfather, who won the race at Newmarket, could have gone faster. When we came to the bridge John pulled me up a little and patted my neck. "Well done, Beauty! Good old fellow," he said.

He would have let me go slower, but my spirit was up, and I was off again as fast as before. The air was frosty, the moon was bright; it was very pleasant. We came through a village, then through a dark wood, then uphill, then downhill, till after eight miles' run we came to the town, through the streets and into the marketplace. It was all quite still except the clatter of my feet on the stones—everybody was asleep. The church clock struck three as we drew up at Dr. White's door.

(1) What did Black Beauty do for two miles?

Black Beauty __________ as fast as he could for two miles.

(2) When they arrived at the bridge, what did John do?

John ________ Black Beauty up and ________ his neck.

(3) Put a check (✓) next to the word that describes Black Beauty's run.

( ) relaxed ( ) sluggish ( ) fast

(4) Describe the route that John and Black Beauty took after the village.

John and Black Beauty went through a _______ wood, then __________, then __________.

(5) Write a **D** next to the sentence below that is description only.

( ) There was a long piece of level road by the river side.
( ) John thumped upon the door.
( ) I galloped as fast as I could for two miles.
( ) The moon was bright.
( ) I was off again as fast as before.
( ) It was very pleasant.
( ) It was all quite still except the clatter of my feet on the stones.
( ) The air was frosty.

1 Read the word problem, and write the number sentence below. Then answer the question. 20 points per question

(1) Jessica's mother weighs 54 kilograms, and that is twice as much as Jessica weighs. Jessica weighs 3 times as much as her baby sister. How much does Jessica's baby sister weigh?

Ans. ______________

(2) There are apples and melons in the fruit basket in the cafeteria. Altogether there are 35 pieces of fruit in the basket. If there are 4 times as many apples as melons, how many of each kind of fruit is in the basket?

Ans. Apples ______ Melons ______

(3) At Farmer William's farm, he has cows and horses. He has 3 times as many horses as cows. If there are 34 more horses than cows, how many of each does Farmer William have?

Ans. Cows ______ Horses ______

(4) Ted has 5 pieces of 8-inch tape, but he connects them so 2 inches overlap. How long is his new piece?

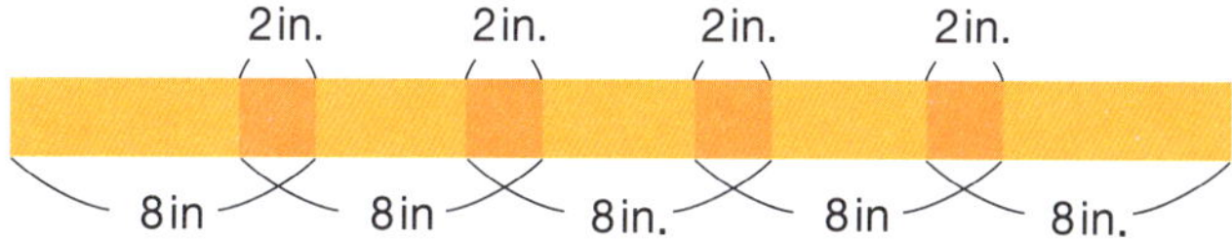

Ans. ______________

(5) Sally's living room is 3 meters and 50 centimeters wide. Her pictures are 35 centimeters wide, and she wants the pictures spaced equally as shown below. How much space should she put between the pictures in her living room?

Ans. ______________

Actions & Descriptions

Black Beauty 3

Date / /

Name

① Read the passage. Then answer the questions below. 25 points per quest

John rang the bell twice, and then knocked at the door like thunder. A window was thrown up, and Dr. White, in his nightcap, put his head out and said, "What do you want?"

"Mrs. Gordon is very ill, sir; master wants you to go at once; he thinks she will die if you cannot get there. Here is a note."

"Wait," he said, "I will come."

He shut the window, and was soon at the door.

"The worst of it is," he said, "that my horse has been out all day and is quite done up; my son has just been sent for, and he has taken the other. What is to be done? Can I have your horse?"

"He has come at a gallop nearly all the way, sir, and I was to give him a rest here; but I think my master would not be against it, if you think fit, sir."

"All right," he said; "I will soon be ready."

John stood by me and stroked my neck; I was very hot. The doctor came out with his riding-whip.

"You need not take that, sir," said John; "Black Beauty will go till he drops. Take care of him, sir, if you can; I should not like any harm to come to him."

"No, no, John," said the doctor, "I hope not," and in a minute we had left John far behind.

(1) What did John do to get the doctor to wake up?

John ________ the bell twice and ________ at the door.

(2) Describe how John knocked at the door.

John knocked at the door like ____________.

(3) While they waited for the doctor, what did John do?

John ____________ Black Beauty's neck.

(4) Write an **A** next to the sentence below that is action only.

( ) John rang the bell twice.
( ) Dr. White's nightcap was droopy.
( ) Dr. White shut the window, and was soon at the door.
( ) John stood by me and stroked my neck.
( ) John knocked at the door.
( ) The knock was like thunder.
( ) I was very hot.
( ) In a minute we had left John far behind.

Way to go!

1 The table and the graph pictured here both show the temperature over the course of one day. Answer the questions about the graph below. 25 points per question

Temperatures Throughout One Day

Time (o'clock)	6	7	8	9	10	11	12	1	2	3	4	5	6
Temperature (℃)	12	14	15	16	18	20	21	22	24	23	20	19	17

(1) Write the appropriate label for the horizontal axis.

(2) Write the appropriate label for the vertical axis.

(3) Complete the line graph by placing each point and then connecting them with a line.

(4) Write the title in A.

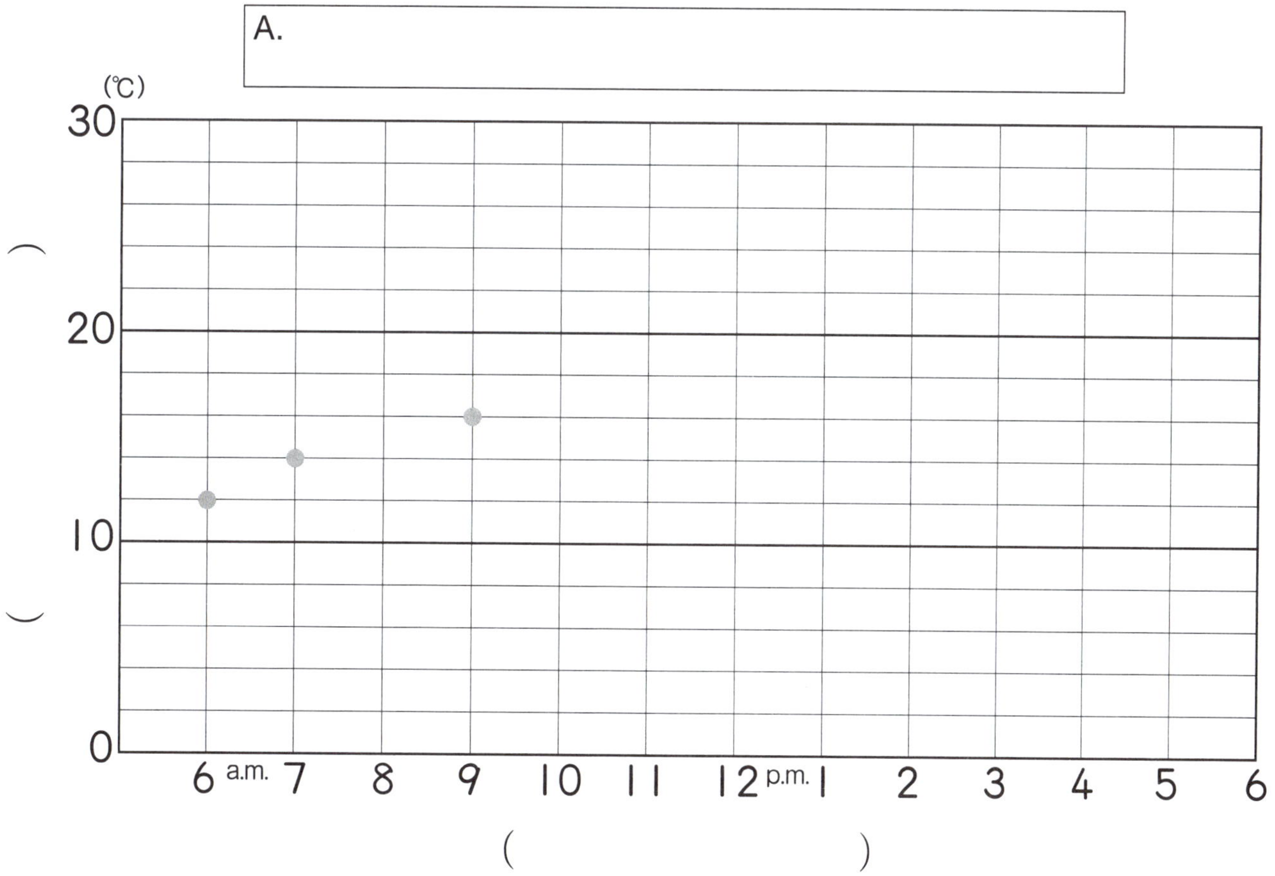

A.

(℃)
30
20
10
0

6 a.m. 7 8 9 10 11 12 p.m. 1 2 3 4 5 6

( )

Actions & Descriptions

Black Beauty 4

Date / / Name

Level ★★ Score /1

① Read the passage. Then answer the questions below. 20 points per ques

I will not tell about our way back. The doctor was a heavier man than John and not so good a rider; however, I did my very best. The man at the toll-gate had it open. When we came to the hill the doctor drew me up. "Now, my good fellow," he said, "take some breath." I was glad he did, for I was nearly spent, but that breathing helped me on, and soon we were in the park. Joe was at the lodge gate; my master was at the hall door, for he had heard us coming. He spoke not a word; the doctor went into the house with him, and Joe led me to the stable. I was glad to get home; my legs shook under me, and I could only stand and pant. I had not a dry hair on my body, the water ran down my legs, and I steamed all over, Joe used to say, like a pot on the fire. Poor Joe! He was young and small, and as yet he knew very little, and his father, who would have helped him, had been sent to the next village; but I am sure he did the very best he knew. He rubbed my legs and my chest, but he did not put my warm cloth on me; he thought I was so hot I should not like it. Then he gave me a pailful of water to drink; it was cold and very good, and I drank it all; then he gave me some hay and some corn, and thinking he had done right, he went away. Soon I began to shake and tremble, and turned deadly cold; my legs ached, my loins ached, and my chest ached, and I felt sore all over. Oh! How I wished for my warm, thick cloth, as I stood and trembled. I wished for John, but he had eight miles to walk, so I lay down in my straw and tried to go to sleep.

(1) How was the doctor different from John?

The doctor was a ___________ man than John and not as ________ a rider.

(2) When they came to the hill, what did the doctor make Black Beauty do?

When they came to the hill, the doctor made Black Beauty take a ___________.

(3) Describe Joe.

Joe was ___________ and __________ and knew ________ about caring for horses.

(4) Write an **A** next to the sentences below that are actions only.

( ) I was like a pot on fire.
( ) I began to shake and tremble.
( ) I lay down in my straw.

(5) Write a **D** next to the sentences below that are descriptions only.

( ) I was glad to get home.
( ) I had not a dry hair on my body.
( ) He rubbed my legs and my chest.

Volume

Date / /

Name

Level ★★

Score /100

Math DAY 31

Don't forget!

The volume of a cube with sides of 1 inch is called 1 cubic inch and is written 1 in.^{3}

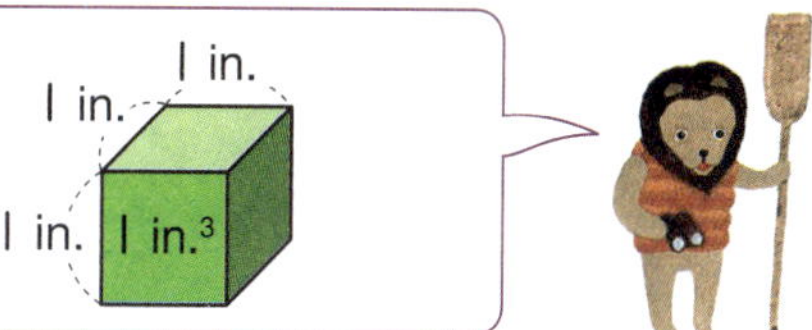

1 The following shapes were made by cubes with 1-inch sides. Calculate the volume of each shape below. 10 points per question

(1)

(1 in.^{3})

(2)

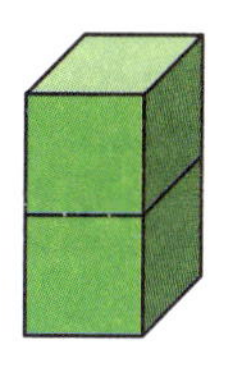

(   )

(3)

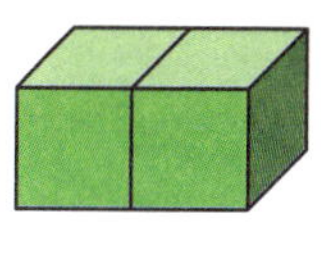

(   )

(4)

(   )

(5)

(   )

2 Calculate the volume of the following rectangular, solid shapes—also called prisms. Answer in cubic inches. 10 points per question

(1)

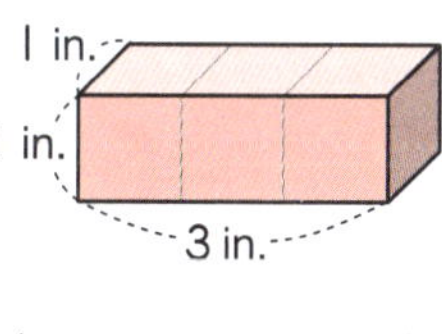

(   )

(2)

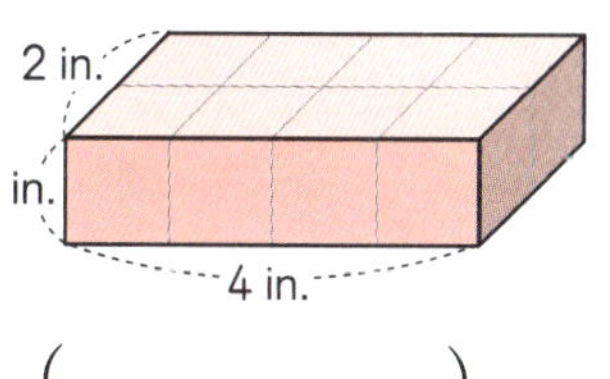

(   )

(3)

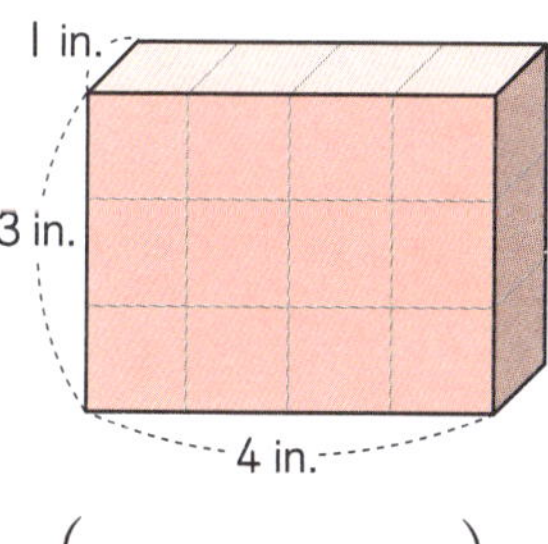

(   )

(4)

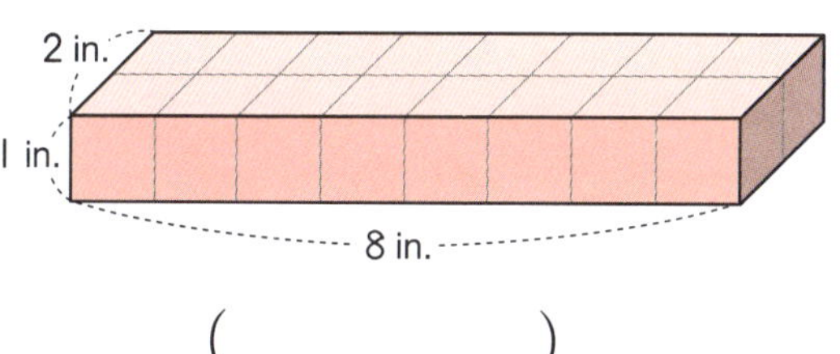

(   )

(5)

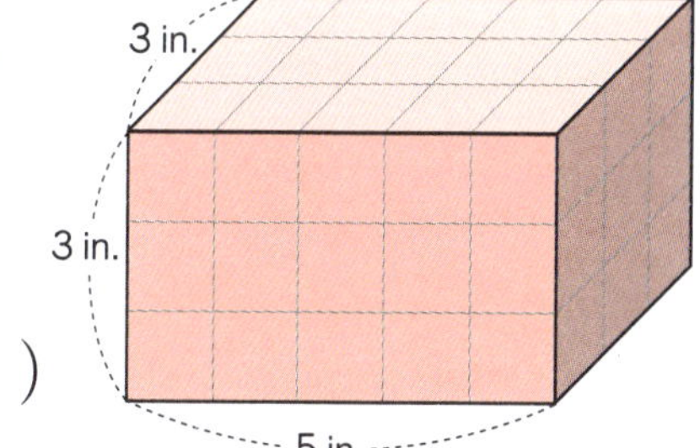

(   )

Reading Comprehension

My Father's Dragon 1

Level ★★

Date / /

Name

Score /1

① Read the excerpt from *My Father's Dragon* by Ruth Stiles Gannett. Then answer the questions below. 20 points per question

The river was very wide and muddy, and the jungle was very gloomy and dense. The trees grew close to each other, and what room there was between them was taken up by great high ferns with sticky leaves. My father hated to leave the beach, but he decided to start along the river bank where at least the jungle wasn't quite so thick. He ate three tangerines, making sure to keep all the peels this time, and put on his rubber boots.

My father tried to follow the river bank but it was very swampy, and as he went farther the swamp became deeper. When it was almost as deep as his boot tops he got stuck in the oozy, mucky mud. My father tugged and tugged, and nearly pulled his boots right off, but at last he managed to wade to a drier place. Here the jungle was so thick that he could hardly see where the river was. He unpacked his compass and figured out the direction he should walk in order to stay near the river. But he didn't know that the river made a very sharp curve away from him just a little way beyond, and so as he walked straight ahead he was getting farther and farther away from the river.

(1) Put a check (✓) next to the phrases that describe the story's setting.

( ) **A dry and hot jungle**
( ) **A gloomy and dense jungle**
( ) **The lobby of a bank**
( ) **A wide and muddy river**
( ) **A river bank**

(2) Who is the story about?

The story is about someone's __________.

(3) Who is telling the story?

The man's _______ or __________ is telling the story.

(4) Why does the father start along the river bank?

He starts along the river bank because the ________ isn't quite so _______ there.

(5) What does the narrator know that the father does not know?

The narrator knows that the river makes a very ______________ and that the father was getting __________ from the river.

Don't forget! The **narrator** is the person who tells the events of a story. The **setting** is the background (specifically the time and place) of a story.

Volume

Level ★★

Date / /

Name

Score /100

Math DAY 32

Don't forget!

The volume of a cube with sides of 1 centimeter is called 1 cubic centimeter and is written 1 cm^3

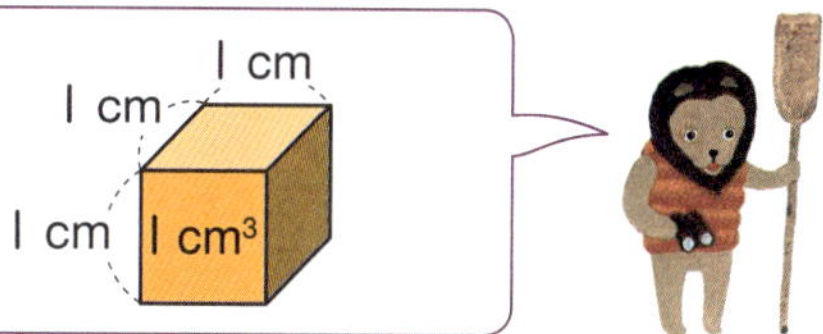

1 The following shapes were made by cubes with 1 cm sides. Calculate the volume of each shape below. 10 points per question

(1)

(I cm^3)

(2)

( )

(3)

( )

(4)

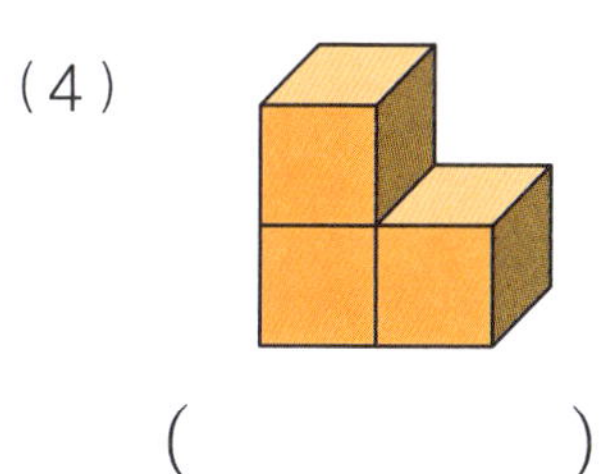

( )

(5)

( )

2 Calculate the volume of the following rectangular, solid shapes—also called prisms. Answer in cubic centimeters. 10 points per question

(1)

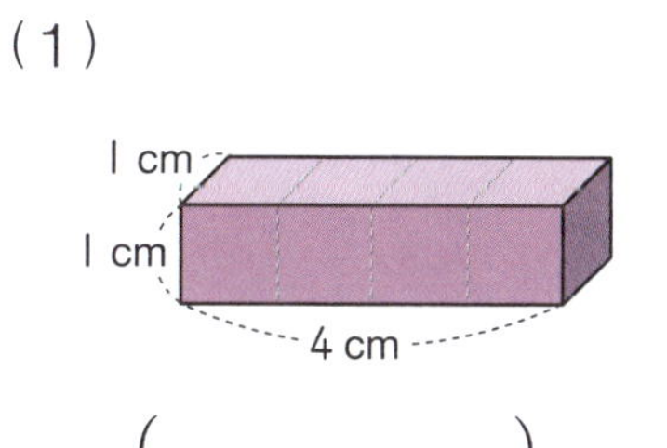

( )

(2)

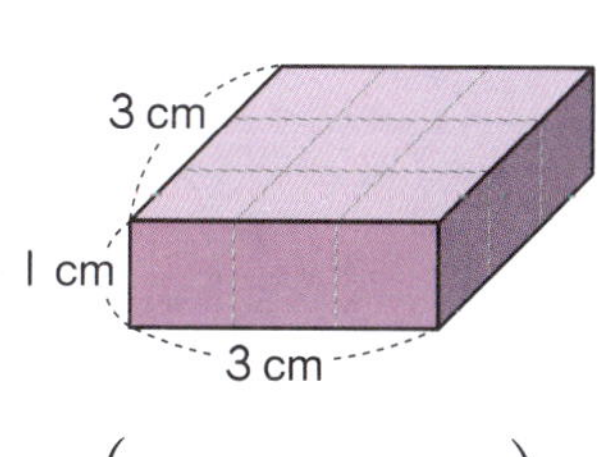

( )

(3)

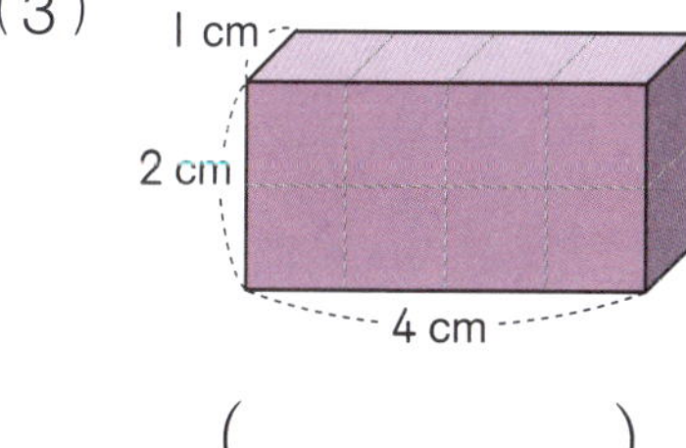

( )

(4)

3 cm

I cm

5 cm

( )

(5)

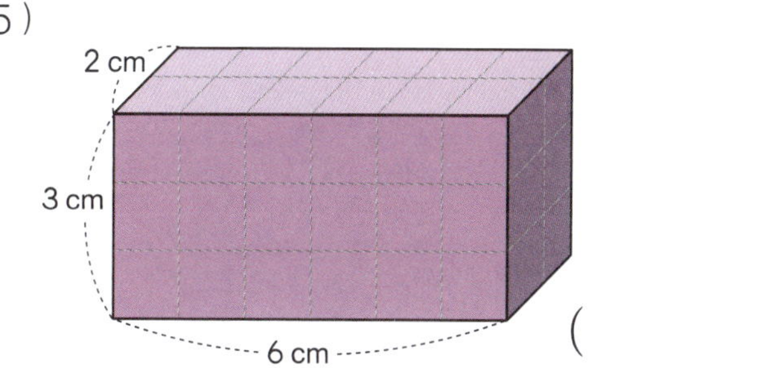

( )

Reading DAY 32

Reading Comprehension

My Father's Dragon 2

Date / /

Name

Level ★★

Score /1

① Read the passage. Then answer the questions below.

It was very hard to walk in the jungle. The sticky leaves of the ferns caught at my father's hair, and he kept tripping over roots and rotten logs. Sometimes the trees were clumped so closely together that he couldn't squeeze between them and had to walk a long way around.

He began to hear whispery noises, but he couldn't see any animals anywhere. The deeper into the jungle he went the surer he was that something was following him, and then he thought he heard whispery noises on both sides of him as well as behind. He tried to run, but he tripped over more roots, and the noises only came nearer. Once or twice he thought he heard something laughing at him.

At last he came out into a clearing and ran right into the middle of it so that he could see anything that might try to attack him. Was he surprised when he looked and saw fourteen green eyes coming out of the jungle all around the clearing, and ten the green eyes turned into seven tigers! The tigers walked around him in a big circle, looking hungrier all the time, and then they sat down and began to talk.

"I suppose you thought we didn't know you were trespassing in our jungle!"

(1) Why was it for the father hard to walk in the jungle? 30 points for com

It was hard to walk in the jungle because the father kept tripping over ________ and ________ .

(2) Complete the chart below that shows the cause of each of the father's actions. 40 points for co

Cause	Effect
The trees were clumped close together.	The father had to ______ a long way around.
The father heard whispery noises all around him.	He tried to ______.
The father wanted to see anything that might try to attack him.	He ______ into the middle of a ________.

(3) What did the tigers think that the father was doing? 30 points

The tigers thought that the father was ________ in their jungle.

Don't forget! The **plot** is the main events of a story that are connected by cause and effect.

Don't forget!

2 cups = 1 pint (pt.) **8 fluid ounces (fl. oz.) = 1 cup**

1 Convert the measurements below. 5 points per question

(1) 1 pt. = ☐ cups

(2) 2 pt. = ☐ cups

(3) 3 pt. = ☐ cups

(4) 2 cups = ☐ pt

(5) 1 cups = ☐ pt.

(6) 4 cups = ☐ pt.

2 Convert the measurements below. 5 points per question

(1) 1 cups = ☐ fl. oz.

(2) 2 cups = ☐ fl. oz.

(3) 4 cups = ☐ fl. oz.

(4) 8 fl. oz. = ☐ cups

(5) 24 fl. oz. = ☐ cups

(6) 40 fl. oz. = ☐ cups

3 How much water is in each measuring cup below? Answer in two different units. 10 points per question

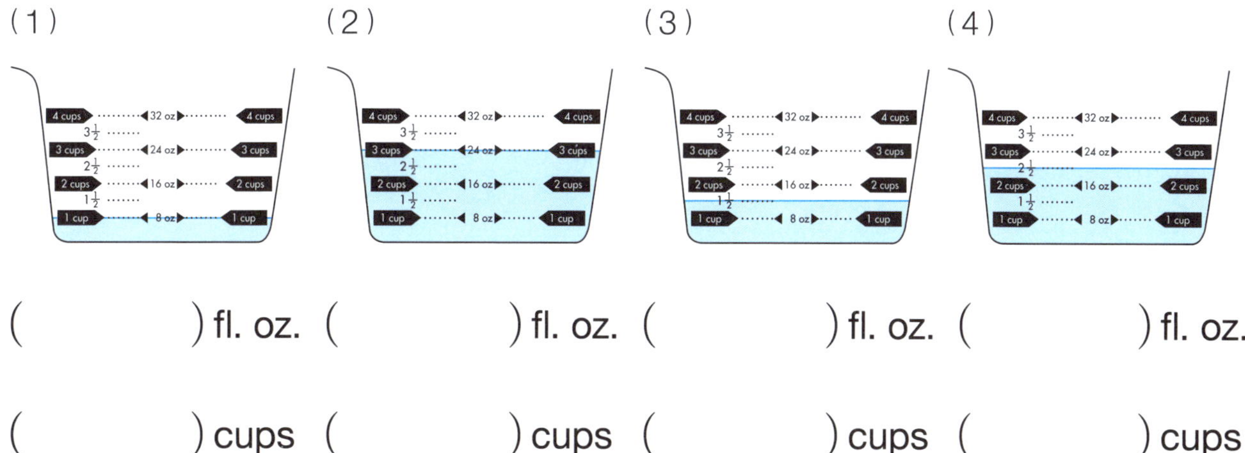

(1) (　　　) fl. oz. (　　　) cups

(2) (　　　) fl. oz. (　　　) cups

(3) (　　　) fl. oz. (　　　) cups

(4) (　　　) fl. oz. (　　　) cups

Reading DAY 33

Reading Comprehension

My Father's Dragon 3

Date / /　Name

Level ★★ Score /

① Read the passage. Then answer the questions below.　100 points for...

Then the next tiger spoke. "I suppose you're going to say you didn't know it was our jungle!"

"Did you know that not one explorer has ever left this island alive?" said the third tiger.

My father thought of the cat* and knew this wasn't true. But of course he had too much sense to say so. One doesn't contradict a hungry tiger.

The tigers went on talking in turn. "You're our first little boy, you know. I'm curious to know if you're especially tender."

"Maybe you think we have regular meal-times, but we don't. We just eat whenever we're feeling hungry," said the fifth tiger.

"And we're very hungry right now. In fact, I can hardly wait," said the sixth.

"I can't wait!" said the seventh tiger.

And then all the tigers said together in a loud roar, "Let's begin right now!" and they moved in closer.

*In an earlier story in My Father's Dragon, the father meets a cat who was an explorer and had visited the island.

(1) Who is talking in this scene?

A group of ________ is talking in this scene.

(2) How many tigers are talking?

There are ________ tigers talking.

(3) What does the third tiger say?

The third tiger says that not one ________ has ever ________ the island alive.

(4) What does the fifth tiger say?

The fifth tiger says that they eat ________ they're feeling hungry.

(5) Does the father reply to the tigers?

________, the father ________ reply to the tiger.

(6) What do the tigers say all together?

The tigers say in a loud roar, " ________________!"

Don't forget! Dialogue is the conversation between two or more characters in a story.

Area

Date / /

Name

Level ★★

Score /100

Math DAY 34

Don't forget!
In order to find the area of a square or rectangle, use the following formulas.
The area of a rectangle = length × width
The area of a square = side × side

1 What is the area of each shape below? Answer in square inches and use the formulas from above. 8 points per question

(1) 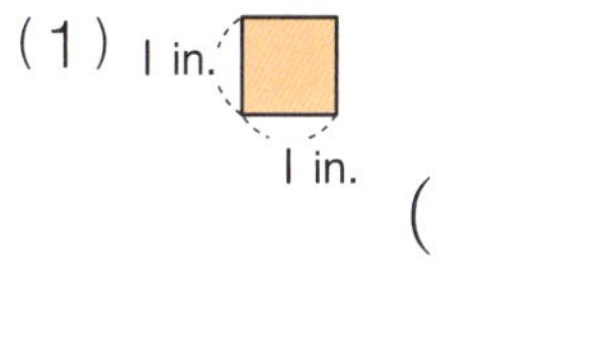

(   )

(2) 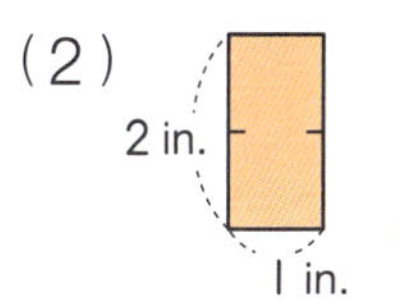

(   )

(3) 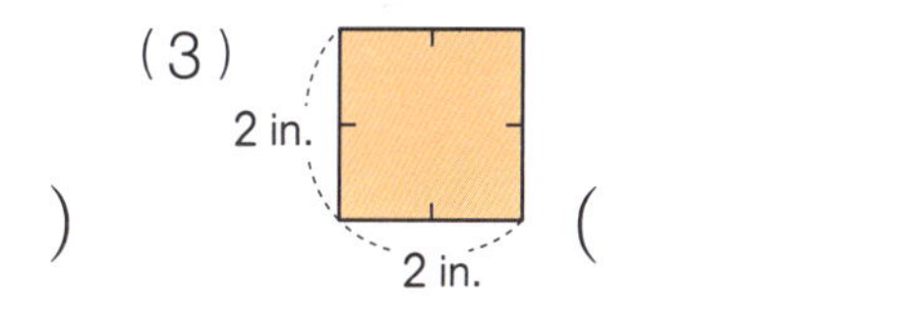

(   )

(4) 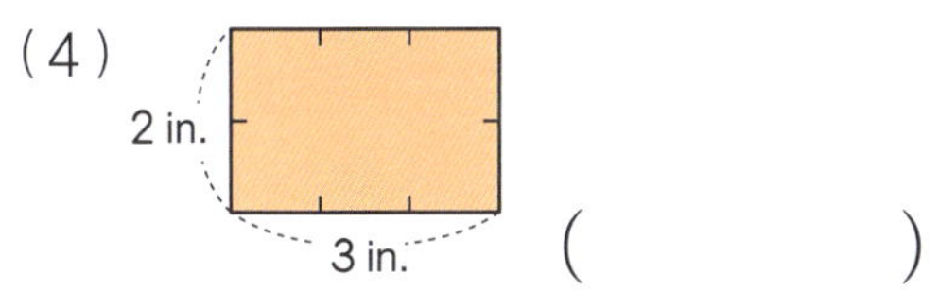

(   )

(5) 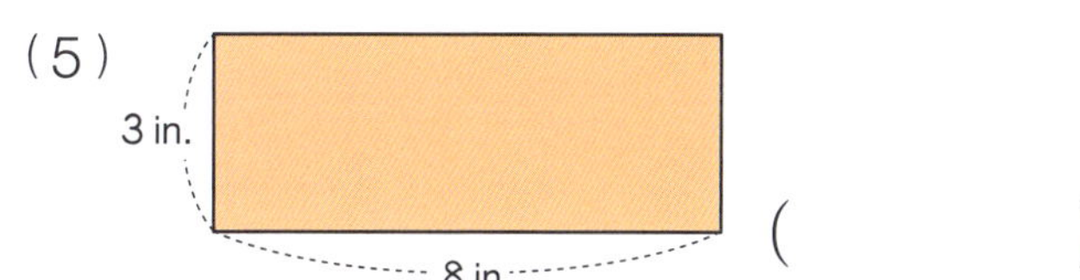

(   )

2 What is the area of each shape below? Answer each unit. 

(1) 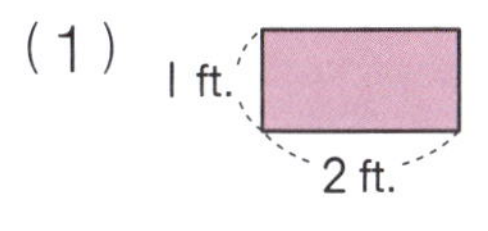

(   )

(2) 

(   )

(3) 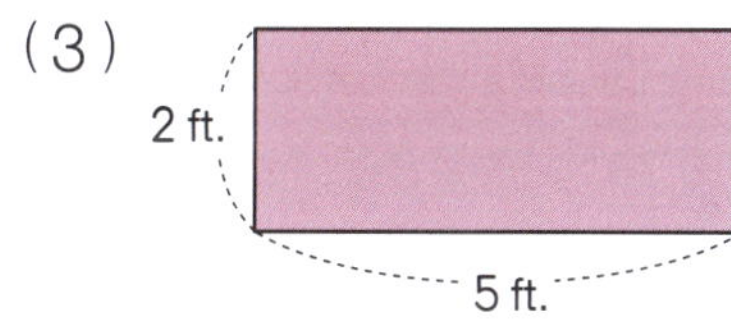

(   )

(4) 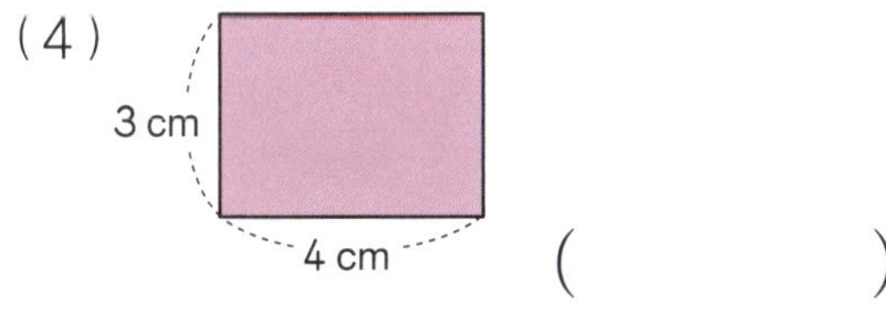

(   )

(5) 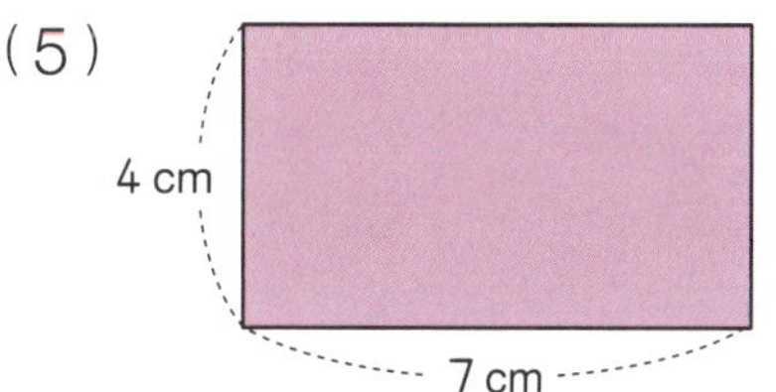

(   )

3 What is the area of each shape below? Answer in square meters. 10 points per question

(1) 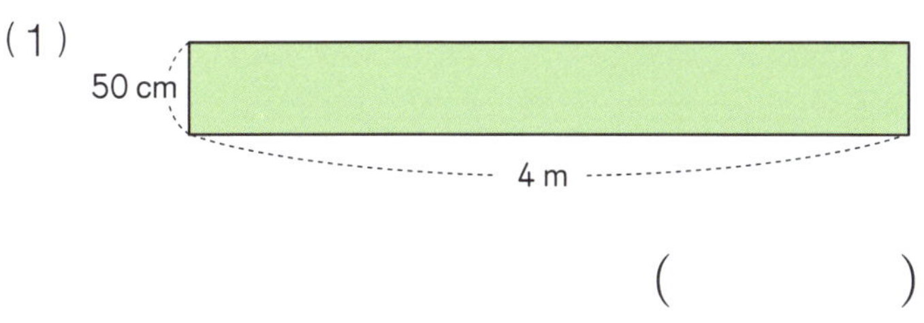

(   )

(2) 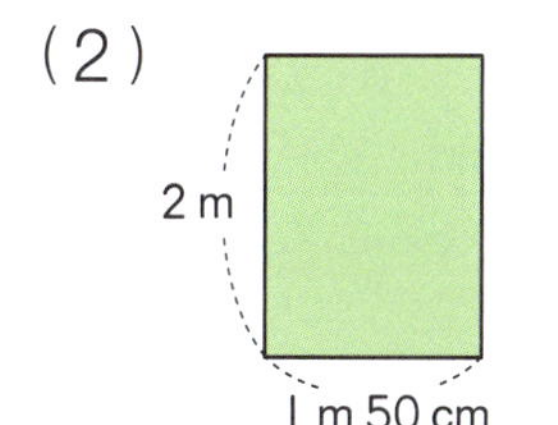

(   )

Reading DAY 34

Reading Comprehension

My Father's Dragon 4

Date / / Name

Level ★★ Score /1

① Read the passage. Then answer the questions below.

My father looked at those seven hungry tigers, and then he had an idea. He quickly opened his knapsack and took out the chewing gum. The cat had told him that tigers were especially fond of chewing gum, which was very scarce on the island. So he threw them each a piece but they only growled, "As fond as we are of chewing gum, we're sure we'd like you even better!" and they moved so close that he could feel them breathing on his face.

"But this is very special chewing gum," said my father. "If you keep on chewing it long enough it will turn green, and then if you plant it, it will grow more chewing gum, and the sooner you start chewing the sooner you'll have more."

The tigers said, "Why, you don't say! Isn't that fine!" And as each one wanted to be the first to plant the chewing gum, they all unwrapped their pieces and began chewing as hard as they could. Every once in a while one tiger would look into another's mouth and say, "Nope, it's not done yet," until finally they were all so busy looking into each other's mouths to make sure that no one was getting ahead that they forgot all about my father.

(1) Why did the father throw each tiger a piece of chewing gum? 25 points

The father threw each tiger a piece of chewing gum because the cat had told him that tigers are especially ____________________.

(2) What was supposedly special about the chewing gum? 25 points for cor

The chewing gum was supposedly special because if you kept chewing it, it would turn__________ and you could __________ it to grow more gum.

(3) Complete the chart below that shows the effect of the father's action. 50 points for cor

Cause	Effect
The father tells the tigers that the chewing gum has special powers.	All the tigers ______________ their gum and began ___________ it as hard as they could.
	The tigers would ________________________ to check if the gum was green.
	The tigers forgot all about the narrator's ________.

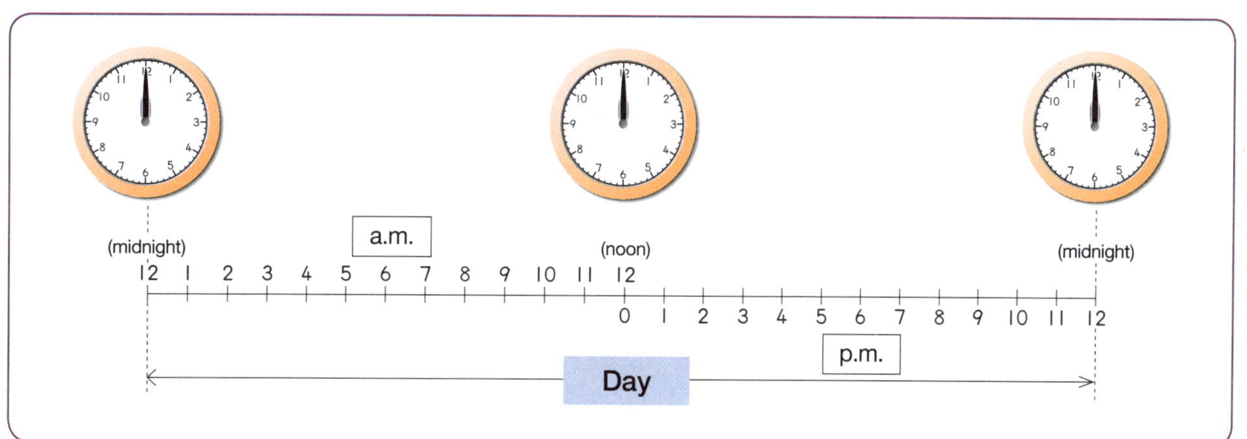

1 Use the figure above in order to answer the questions below. 10 points per question

(1) The short hand moves all the way around the clock once from [ ] to noon.

(2) The short hand moves all the way around the clock once from noon to [ ].

(3) The short hand moves all the way around the clock once every [ ] hour(s).

(4) The short hand moves all the way around the clock [ ] times in one day.

(5) [ ] hours pass between midnight and 8 a.m.

(6) 9 hours after midnight, the time is [ ] a.m.

2 Answer the questions below using the clock pictured here. 10 points per question

(1) Half an hour ago ( )

(2) Half an hour from now ( )

(3) An hour ago ( )

(4) An hour from now ( )

Reading DAY 35

Reading Comprehension

"My Shadow"

Level ★★

Date / / Name Score /100

1 Read the poem "My Shadow" by Robert Louis Stevenson. Then answer the questions below. 25 points per question

I have a little shadow that goes in and out with me,
And what can be the use of him is more than I can see.
He is very, very like me from the heels up to the head;
And I see him jump before me, when I jump into my bed.

The funniest thing about him is the way he likes to grow—
Not at all like proper children, which is always very slow;
For he sometimes shoots up taller like an india-rubber ball,
And he sometimes gets so little that there's none of him at all.

He hasn't got a notion of how children ought to play,
And can only make a fool of me in every sort of way.
He stays so close beside me, he's a coward, you can see;
I'd think shame to stick to nursie as that shadow sticks to me!

One morning, very early, before the sun was up,
I rose and found the shining dew on every buttercup;
But my lazy little shadow, like an arrant* sleepy-head,
Had stayed at home behind me and was fast asleep in bed.

*"Arrant" means complete or utter.

(1) Which words in the first stanza rhyme with each other?

Me rhymes with ________, and ________ rhymes with ________.

(2) Which words in the second stanza rhyme with each other?

________ rhymes with ________, and ________ rhymes with ________.

(3) Put a check (✓) next to the phrases that describe the shadow in the poem.

( ) a copy-cat
( ) shaped like the person
( ) always wandering away
( ) grows and shrinks slowly
( ) stays close
( ) sleeps all the time

(4) Put a check (✓) next to the phrases that describe some of the poem's main ideas.

( ) shadows follow you
( ) shadows are lazy
( ) shadows change
( ) shadows are like the sun
( ) shadows are good at games
( ) your shadow is like you

Don't forget! A **stanza** is a group of lines that usually have a repeating pattern of rhythm and rhyme

Elapsed Time

Date / /

Name

Level ★★

Score /100

1 How much time has passed from the time on the left to the time on the right? 10 points per question

(1) (a.m.) (a.m.)

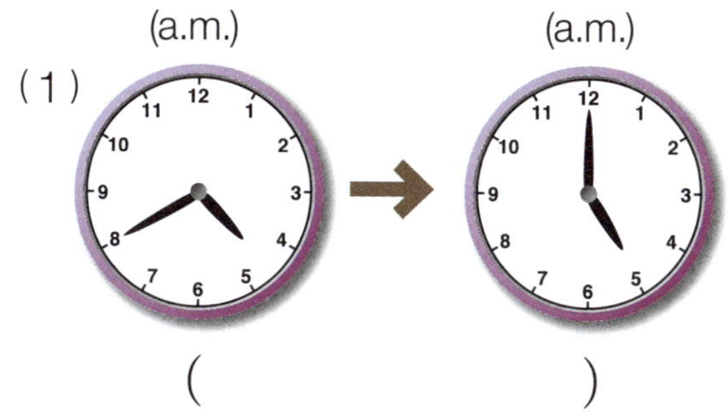

( )

(2) (p.m.) (p.m.)

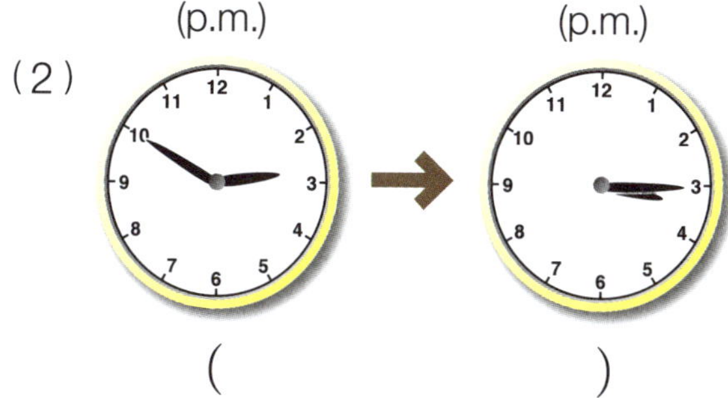

( )

(3) (a.m.) (a.m.)

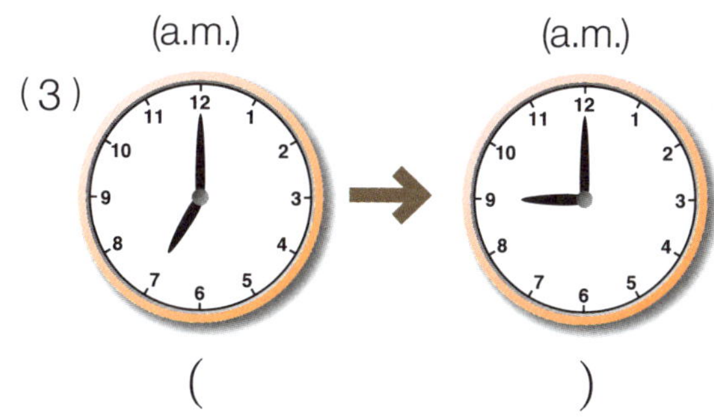

( )

(4) (p.m.) (p.m.)

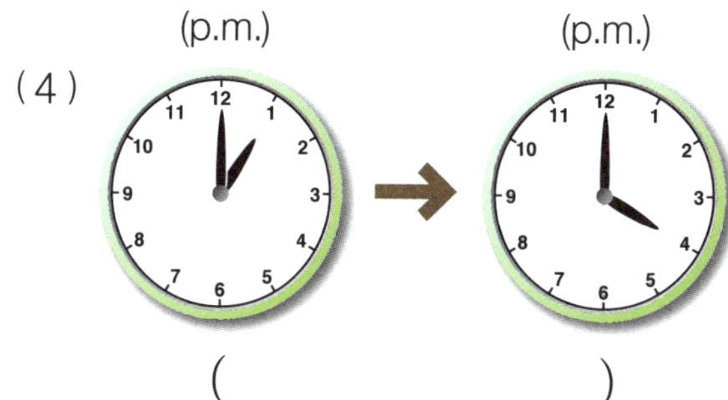

( )

2 How much time has passed from the time on the left to the time on the right? 15 points per question

(1) (a.m.) (a.m.)

( )

(2) (p.m.) (p.m.)

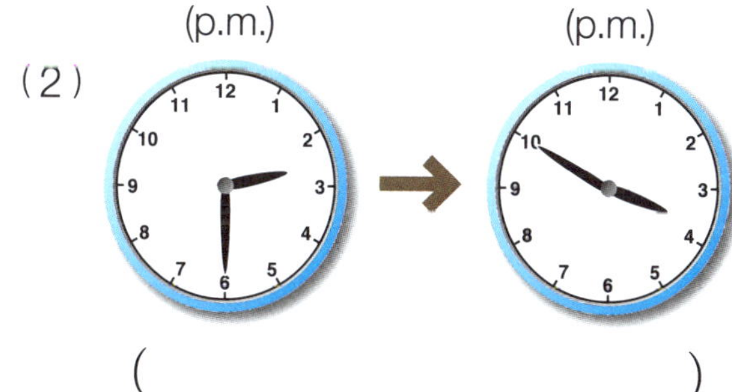

( )

(3) (a.m.) (a.m.)

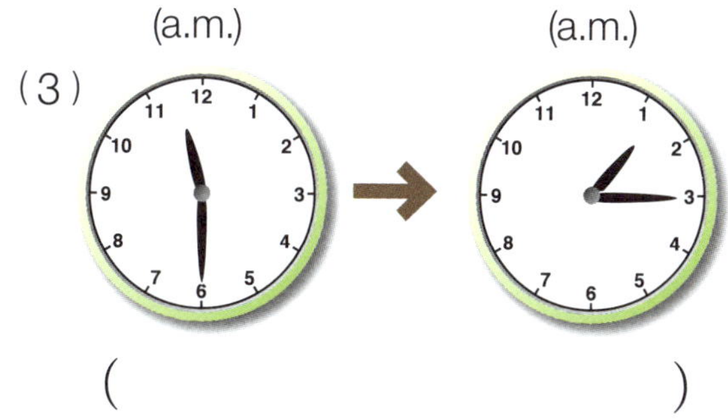

( )

(4) (p.m.) (p.m.)

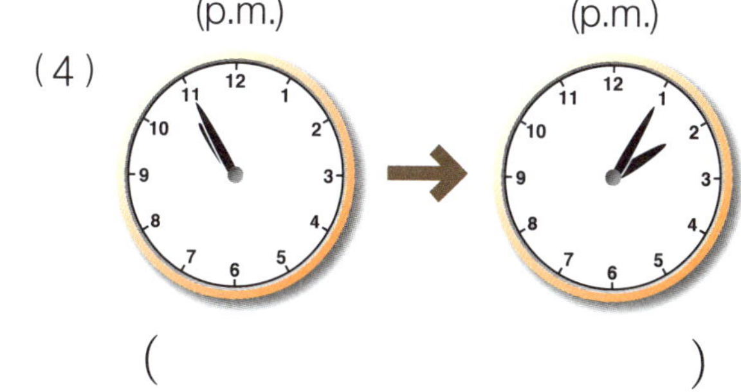

( )

Reading DAY 36

Reading Comprehension

"The Brook"

Date / /

Name

Level ★★

Score /10

① Read the excerpt from the poem "The Brook" by Alfred Tennyson. Then answer the questions below.

I chatter, chatter, as I flow
To join the brimming river;
For men may come and men may go,
But I go on forever.

I wind about, and in and out,
With here a blossom sailing,
And here and there a lusty trout,
And here and there a grayling.

I steal by lawns and grassy plots,
I slide by hazel covers;
I move the sweet forget-me-nots
That grow for happy lovers.

I slip, I slide, I gloom, I glance,
Among my skimming swallows;
I make the netted sunbeams dance
Against my sandy shallows.

I murmur under moon and stars
In brambly wildernesses;
I linger by my shingly bars;
I loiter round my cresses.

And out again I curve and flow
To join the brimming river;
For men may come and men may go,
But I go on forever.

(1) Which words in the second stanza rhyme? 15 points for com

About **rhymes with** ______,

______ **rhymes with** ______,

______ **rhymes with** ______ **and**

______ **rhymes with** ______.

(2) Identify the sounds being repeated in the following examples of alliteration. 15 points for com

"I slip, I slide" sl

"I gloom, I glance" ______

"Among my skimming swallows" ______

(3) What phrase is repeated in the poem? 15 points

The phrase "For men ______

______

______ **is repeated.**

(4) What is speaking in the poem? 15 points

A ______ **is speaking.**

(5) What will the brook join? 15 points

The brook will join the ______.

(6) Put a check (✓) next to the phrases that describe some of the poem's main ideas. 25 points for cor

( ) a brook is long-lasting
( ) a brook can flood
( ) a brook is lively
( ) a brook and ponds are alike
( ) a brook flows far and wide
( ) a brook dries up

Don't forget! Alliteration is the repetition of a sound at the beginning of two or more words close to each other.

Don't forget!

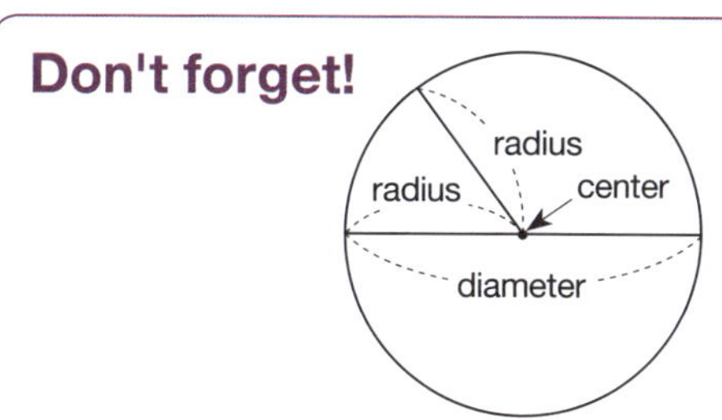

A segment that connects two points on the circle through the center is called the **diameter**.
A segment that connects the center of a circle to any point on the circle is called the **radius**.
The length of the diameter is the radius times two.

1 Write the appropriate number in each box below. 15 points per question

(1) If the radius of a circle is 2 centimeters, its diameter is ☐ centimeters.

(2) If the diameter of a circle is 2 centimeters, its radius is ☐ centimeter(s).

(3) If the radius of a circle is 6 centimeters, its diameter is ☐ centimeters.

(4) If the diameter of a circle is 6 centimeters, its radius is ☐ centimeters.

2 Use a compass to draw a circle in each box below. 20 points per question

(1) Draw a circle with a radius of 2 centimeters.

(2) Draw a circle with a diameter of 5 centimeters.

Reading Comprehension

The Story of Doctor Dolittle 1

Date / / Name

Level ★★ Score /100

1 Read the excerpt from *The Story of Doctor Dolittle* by Hugh Lofting. Then answer the questions below. 100 points for completion

Once upon a time, many years ago when our grandfathers were little children—there was a doctor; and his name was Dolittle—John Dolittle, M.D. "M.D." means that he was a proper doctor and knew a whole lot.

He lived in a little town called Puddleby-on-the-Marsh. All the folks, young and old, knew him well by sight. And whenever he walked down the street in his high hat everyone would say, "There goes the Doctor!—He's a clever man." And the dogs and the children would all run up and follow behind him; and even the crows that lived in the church-tower would caw and nod their heads.

The house he lived in, on the edge of the town, was quite small; but his garden was very large and had a wide lawn and stone seats and weeping-willows hanging over. His sister, Sarah Dolittle, was housekeeper for him; but the Doctor looked after the garden himself.

He was very fond of animals and kept many kinds of pets. Besides the goldfish in the pond at the bottom of his garden, he had rabbits in the pantry, white mice in his piano, a squirrel in the linen closet and a hedgehog in the cellar. He had a cow with a calf too, and an old lame horse—twenty-five years of age—and chickens, and pigeons, and two lambs, and many other animals. But his favorite pets were Dab-Dab the duck, Jip the dog, Gub-Gub the baby pig, Polynesia the parrot, and the owl Too-Too.

(1) When does the story take place?

The story takes place many __________ ago.

(2) Who is the main character?

____________________ is the main character.

(3) What is the setting of the story?

The setting of the story is the __________ of Dr. Dolittle at the edge of a little town called ________________________________ .

(4) What does Dr. Dolittle's sister, Sarah Dolittle, do?

Sarah Dolittle is Dr. Dolittle's __________________.

(5) Why does Dr. Dolittle keep so many pets?

Dr. Dolittle keeps so many pets because he is very ________________________.

(6) Who are Dr. Dolittle's favorite pets?

Dr. Dolittle's favorite pets are ____________________________, ____________________,

__________________________________, ______________ ______________, and

_______________________.

(7) Why does everyone think Dr. Dolittle is a clever man?

Everyone thinks Dr. Dolittle is a clever man because he is a __________.

1 Two circles of the same size are inside a larger circle that has a radius of 3 inches. 10 points per question

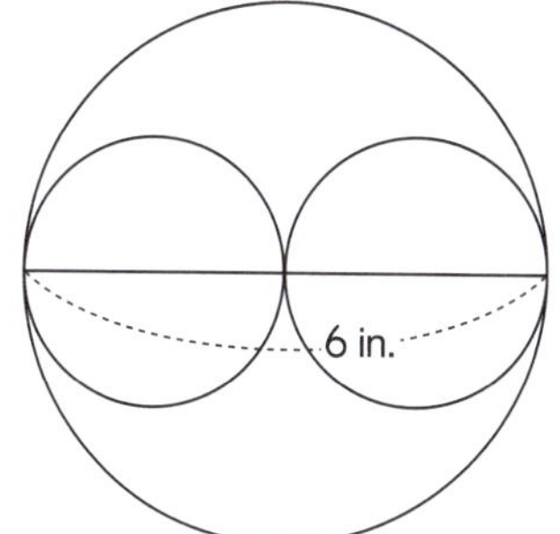

(1) What is the diameter of the big circle? (   )

(2) What is the diameter of each small circle? (   )

(3) What is the radius of each small circle? (   )

2 The radius of the smallest circle in the figure below is 3 centimeters. How long is each side of the square? 35 points

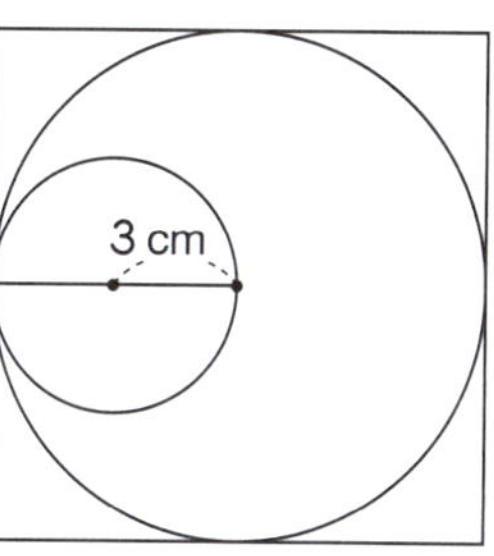

(   )

3 Each circle in the figure below has a radius of 4 inches. How long is the line from A to B? 35 points

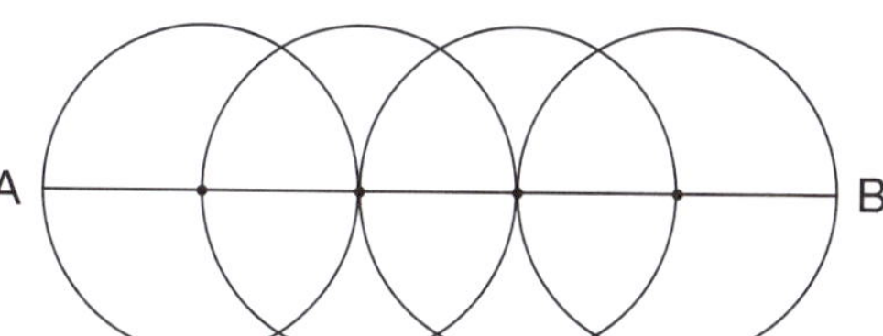

(   )

Reading Comprehension

The Story of Doctor Dolittle 2

Date / / Name

Level ★★ Score /100

① Read the passage. Then answer the questions below. 25 points per question

His sister used to grumble about all these animals and said they made the house untidy. And one day when an old lady with rheumatism came to see the Doctor, she sat on the hedgehog who was sleeping on the sofa and never came to see him anymore, but drove every Saturday all the way to Oxenthorpe, another town ten miles off, to see a different doctor.

Then his sister, Sarah Dolittle, came to him and said, "John, how can you expect sick people to come and see you when you keep all these animals in the house? It's a fine doctor would have his parlor full of hedgehogs and mice! That's the fourth personage these animals have driven away. Squire Jenkins and the Parson say they wouldn't come near your house again—no matter how sick they are. We are getting poorer every day. If you go on like this, none of the best people will have you for a doctor."

"But I like the animals better than the 'best people'," said the Doctor.

"You are ridiculous," said his sister, and walked out of the room.

So, as time went on, the Doctor got more and more animals; and the people who came to see him got less and less. Till at last he had no one left—except the Cat's-meat-Man, who didn't mind any kind of animal. But the Cat's-meat-Man wasn't very rich and he only got sick once a year—at Christmas-time, when he used to give the Doctor sixpence for a bottle of medicine.

(1) Why did Sarah grumble about all the Doctor's animals?

Sarah grumble about the animals because she said they ______________.

(2) Why did the old lady with rheumatism never come back to the Doctor?

The old lady never came back because she accidentally ______________.

(3) Complete the chart with words from the passage above.

Cause	Effect
Because the old lady sat on the hedgehog	She drove all the way to ______________ to see a different ______________.
Because of the Doctor's pets	Less and less ______________ ______________
Because the Cat's-meat-Man didn't mind ______________	He would still visit Doctor Dolittle when he was sick.

(4) What is the main idea of this passage?

The main idea of the passage is: Because Doctor Dolittle got more and more ______________, he got ______________ patients.

Circles & Spheres

Level ★★

Date / /

Name

Score /100

Math DAY 39

Don't forget!

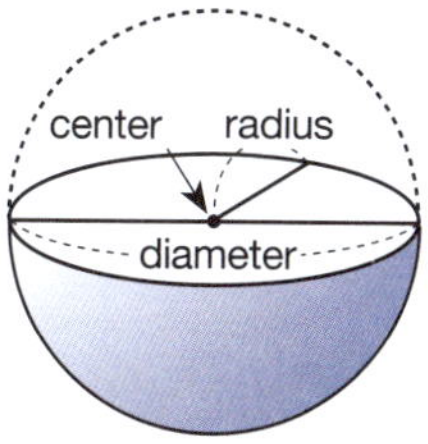

center radius diameter

When you cut a sphere in half, the center, radius and diameter of the circle in its cross section are the center, radius and diameter of the sphere.

1 Write the appropriate number in each box below. 10 points per question

(1) If the diameter of a sphere is 6 centimeters, its radius is ☐ centimeters.

(2) If the diameter of a sphere is 5 centimeters,

its radius is ☐ centimeters and ☐ millimeters.

(3) If the radius of a sphere is 4 centimeters, the diameter is ☐ centimeters.

(4) If the radius of a sphere is 5 centimeters, the diameter is ☐ centimeters.

2 As pictured on the right, you have a sphere that fits snugly inside a box. 12 points per question

(1) How long is each side of the box? ( )

(2) How long is the diameter of the sphere? ( )

(3) How long is the radius of the sphere? ( )

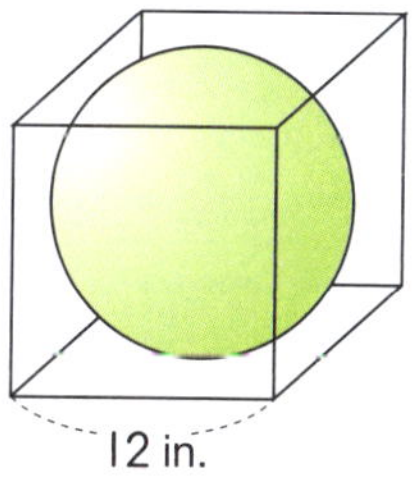

12 in.

3 As pictured on the right, you have six similar balls that fit snugly inside one box that is 15 inches wide. 12 points per question

(1) What is the diameter of each ball? ( )

(2) What is the length of the box? ( )

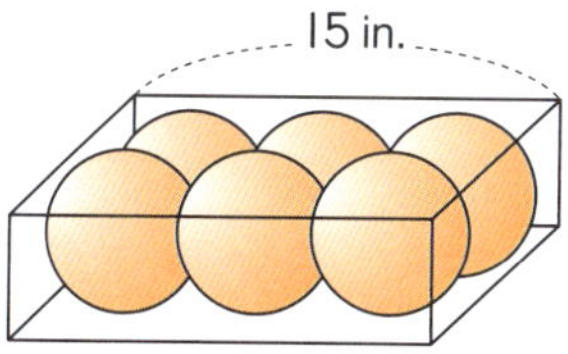

15 in.

Reading Comprehension

The Story of Doctor Dolittle 3

Level ★★

Date / / Name

Score /10

① Read the passage. Then answer the questions below.

Sixpence a year wasn't enough to live on—even in those days, long ago; and if the Doctor hadn't had some money saved up in his money-box, no one knows what would have happened.

And he kept on getting still more pets; and of course it cost a lot to feed them. And the money he had saved up grew littler and littler.

Then he sold his piano, and let the mice live in a bureau-drawer. But the money he got for that too began to go, so he sold the brown suit he wore on Sundays and went on becoming poorer and poorer.

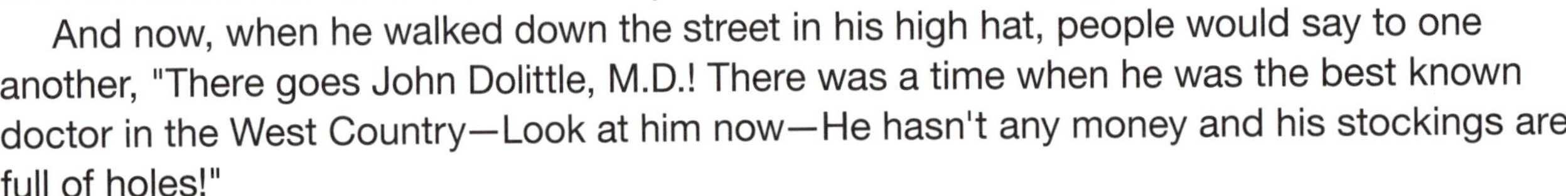

And now, when he walked down the street in his high hat, people would say to one another, "There goes John Dolittle, M.D.! There was a time when he was the best known doctor in the West Country—Look at him now—He hasn't any money and his stockings are full of holes!"

But the dogs and the cats and the children still ran up and followed him through the town—the same as they had done when he was rich.

(1) Complete the chart with words from the passage above.15 points per question — 60 points for cor

Cause	Effect
Sixpence a year wasn't enough to live on.	The doctor spent his __________ money.
He kept on getting still more pets.	The doctor sold ______________.
The money from his piano wasn't enough.	The doctor sold his ______________ and became ______________________.

(2) Identify the statements as **T** (true) or **F** (false) according to the passage. — 10 points per qu

(1) The mice began living in the Doctor's bureau-drawer. **T** **F**

(2) Sixpence a year was just enough to live on. **T** **F**

(3) The Doctor kept losing his pets. **T** **F**

(3) Who didn't care that Doctor Dolittle didn't have any money? — 10 points for cor

The ______ and the ______ and the ____________ didn't care that Doctor Dolittle didn't have any money.

Triangles

Date / /

Name

Don't forget!

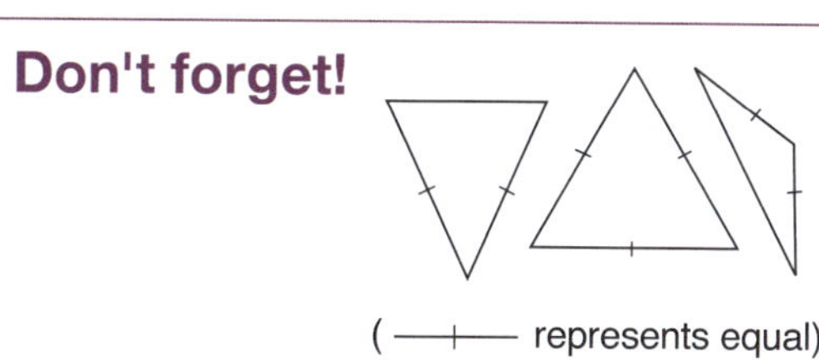

Congruent means equal in size and shape.
A triangle with two congruent sides is an **isosceles** triangle.
A triangle with three congruent sides is called an **equilateral** triangle.

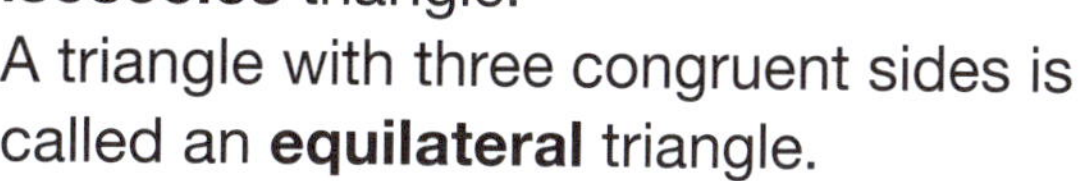

1 Sort the triangles below into equilateral and isosceles triangles by putting each letter next to the correct category. 20 points per question

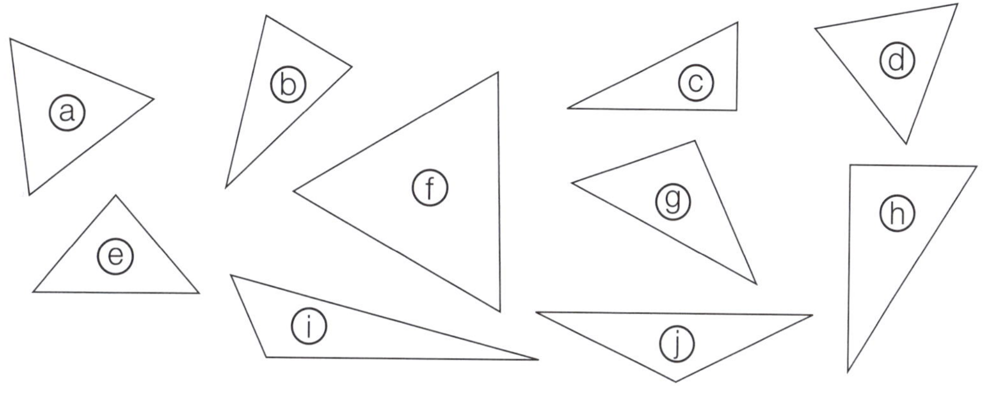

(1) equilateral triangle ( ) (2) isosceles triangle ( )

2 Use your ruler and compass to draw the triangles below. 30 points per question

(1) Draw a triangle with sides that are 4 centimeters, 2 centimeters, and 4 centimeters long.

(2) Draw a triangle with sides that are all 3 centimeters long.

Reading Comprehension

The Story of Doctor Dolittle 4

Date / / Name

Level ★★ Score /100

① Read the passage. Then answer the questions below. 20 points per question

It happened one day that the Doctor was sitting in his kitchen talking with the Cat's-meat-Man who had come to see him with a stomach-ache.

"Why don't you give up being a people's doctor, and be an animal-doctor?" asked the Cat's-meat-Man.

The parrot, Polynesia, was sitting in the window looking out at the rain and singing a sailor-song to herself. She stopped singing and started to listen.

"You see, Doctor," the Cat's-meat-Man went on, "you know all about animals—much more than what these here vets do. That book you wrote—about cats, why, it's wonderful! I can't read or write myself—or maybe I'd write some books. But my wife, Theodosia, she's a scholar, she is. And she read your book to me. Well, it's wonderful—that's all can be said—wonderful. You might have been a cat yourself. You know the way they think. And listen: you can make a lot of money doctoring animals. Do you know that? You see, I'd send all the old women who had sick cats or dogs to you. And if they didn't get sick fast enough, I could put something in the meat I sell 'em to make 'em sick, see?"

"Oh, no," said the Doctor quickly. "You mustn't do that. That wouldn't be right."

"Oh, I didn't mean real sick," answered the Cat's-meat-Man. "Just a little something to make them droopy-like was what I had reference to. But as you say, maybe it ain't quite fair on the animals. But they'll get sick anyway, because the old women always give 'em too much to eat. And look, all the farmers 'round about who had lame horses and weak lambs—they'd come. Be an animal-doctor."

(1) Who is speaking in this passage?

The ____________ and the ________ are speaking in this passage.

(2) Who is listening in this scene?

The ____________ is listening.

(3) What is the Cat's-meat-Man's idea?

The Cat's-meat-Man's idea is that the Doctor should become an ____________.

(4) What are some supporting details for Cat's-meat-Man's suggestion?

(a) The Doctor knows all about ________.

(b) The Doctor wrote a wonderful ________ about ______.

(c) The Doctor can make a lot of ________ doctoring animals.

(5) What does the Doctor tell the Cat's-meat-Man not to do?

The Doctor tells him not to put something in the ______ to make the animals ______.

Reading is fun!

Don't forget!
An **angle** is the geometric figure formed by two distinct rays that have one common endpoint. This common endpoint is called the **vertex** and the rays are called the **sides** of the angle. The measure of an angle is the size of the space between those two distinct rays that have one common end point.

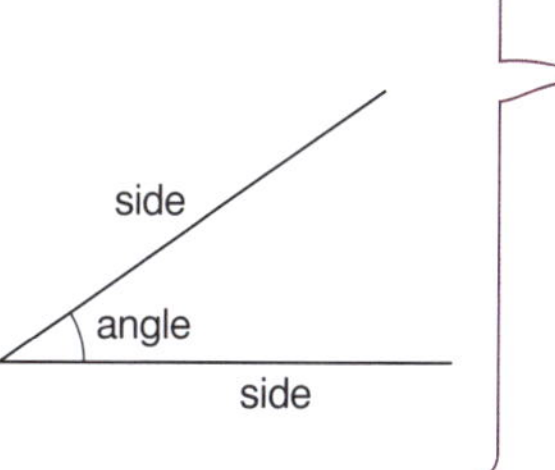

1 Use the protractors to measure each angle below. 10 points per question

(1)

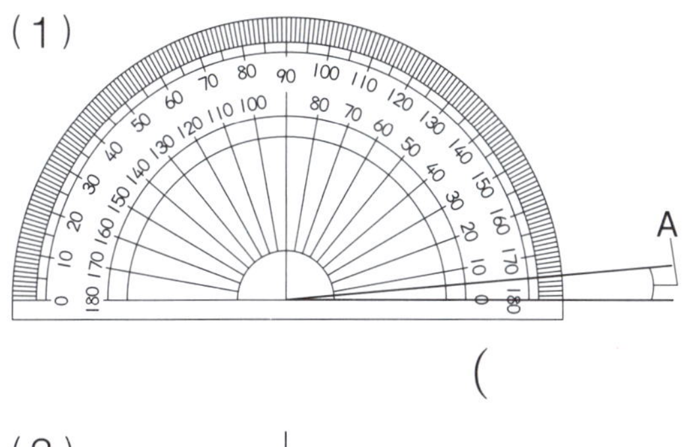

( )

(2)

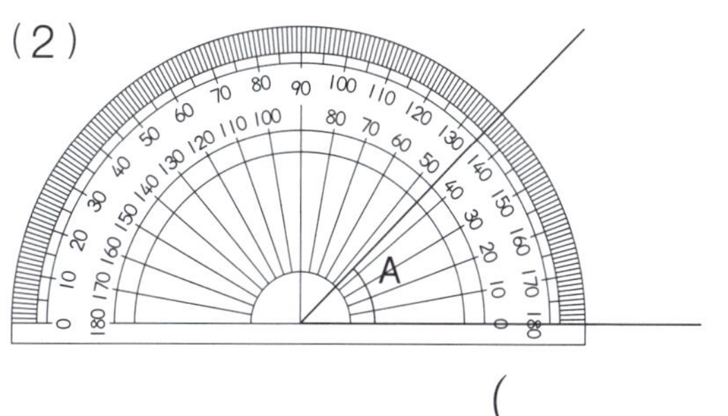

( )

(3)

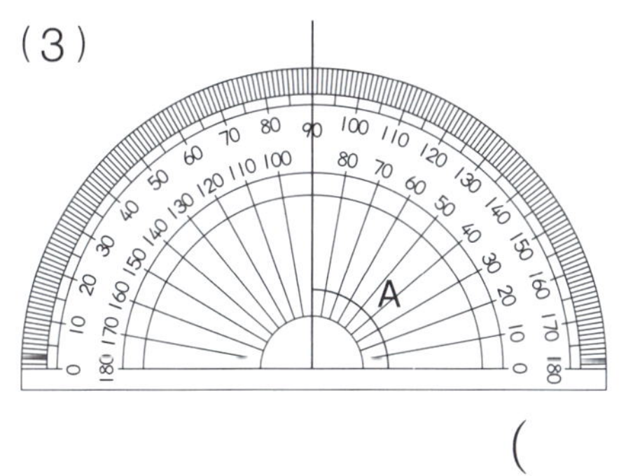

( )

(4)

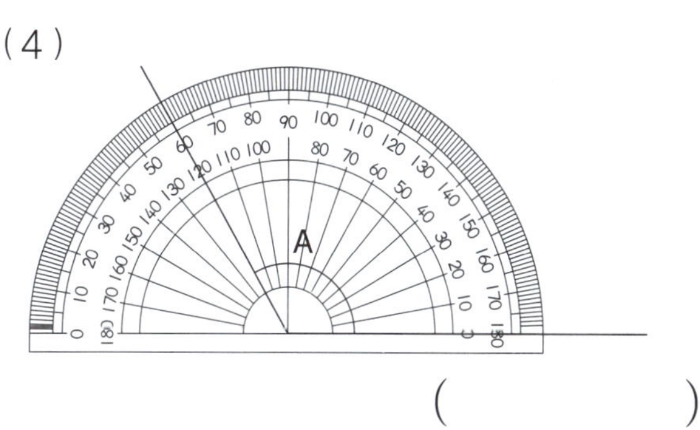

( )

2 Use your own protractor to measure the angles below. 15 points per question

(1)

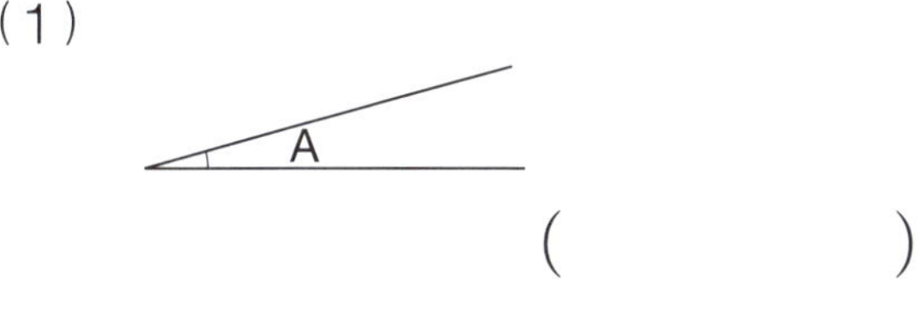

( )

(2)

( )

(3)

( )

(4)

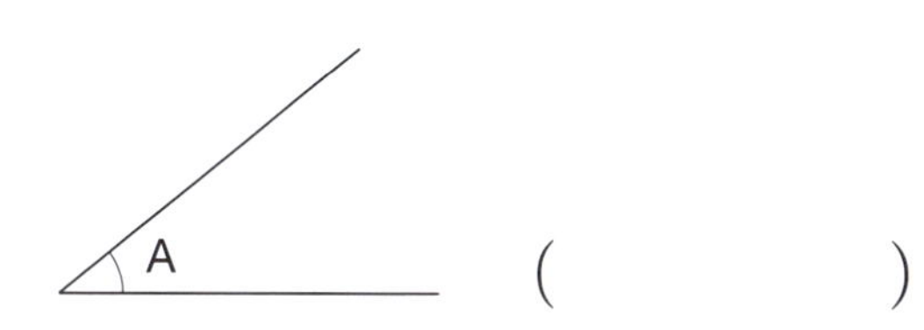

( )

Reading DAY 41

Reading Comprehension

The Story of Doctor Dolittle 5

Date / /

Name

Level ★★

Score

/1

1 Read the passage. Then answer the questions below.

20 points per ques

When the Cat's-meat-Man had gone the parrot flew off the window on to the Doctor's table and said, "That man's got sense. That's what you ought to do. Be an animal-doctor. Give the silly people up—if they haven't brains enough to see you're the best doctor in the world. Take care of animals instead—They'll soon find it out. Be an animal-doctor."

"Oh, there are plenty of animal-doctors," said John Dolittle, putting the flower-pots outside on the window sill to get the rain.

"Yes, there ARE plenty," said Polynesia. "But none of them are any good at all. Now listen, Doctor, and I'll tell you something. Did you know that animals can talk?"

"I knew that parrots can talk," said the Doctor.

"Oh, we parrots can talk in two languages—people's language and bird-language," said Polynesia proudly. "If I say, 'Polly wants a cracker,' you understand me. But hear this: Ka-ka oi-ee, fee-fee?"

"Good gracious!" cried the Doctor. "What does that mean?"

"That means, 'Is the porridge hot yet?'—in bird-language."

"My! You don't say so!" said the Doctor. "You never talked that way to me before."

"What would have been the good?" said Polynesia, dusting some cracker-crumbs off her left wing. "You wouldn't have understood me if I had."

"Tell me some more," said the Doctor, all excited; and he rushed over to the dresser-drawer and came back with the butcher's book and a pencil. "Now don't go too fast—and I'll write it down. This is interesting—very interesting—something quite new. Give me the Birds' ABCs first—slowly now."

(1) Who is speaking this passage?

The ________ and the ________ are speaking in the passage.

(2) What languages does Polynesia speak?

Polynesia speaks ____________ and __________.

(3) Why didn't Polynesia talk to the Doctor in bird-language before?

Polynesia didn't talk to the Doctor in bird-language before because he

__________________.

(4) Why is the Doctor excited?

The Doctor is excited because he is going to learn __________.

(5) How does the Doctor start to learn bird-language?

The Doctor starts by learning the __________ first.

1 Review the example. Then find angle A in each illustration below. 10 points per question

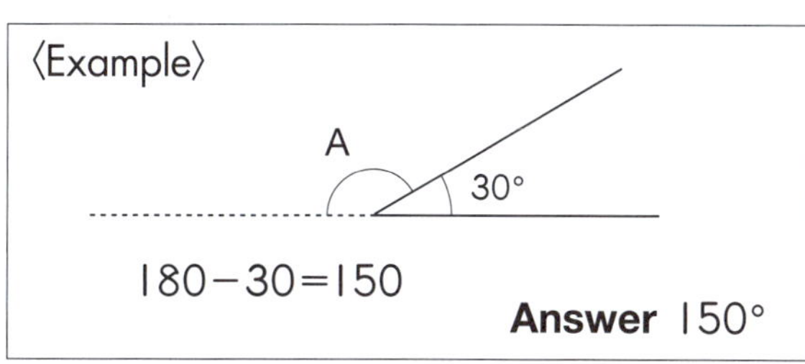

(1)

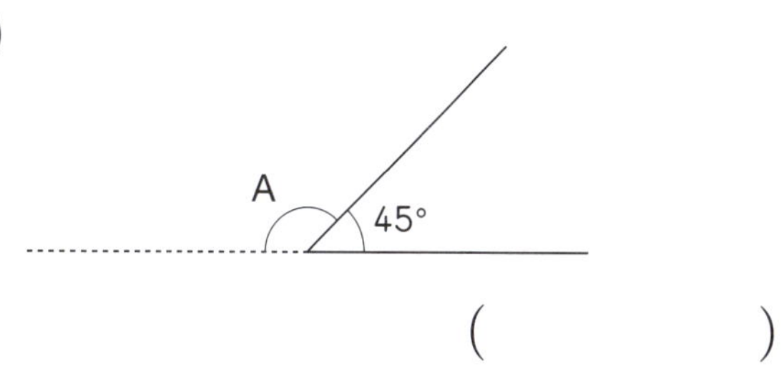

( )

(2)

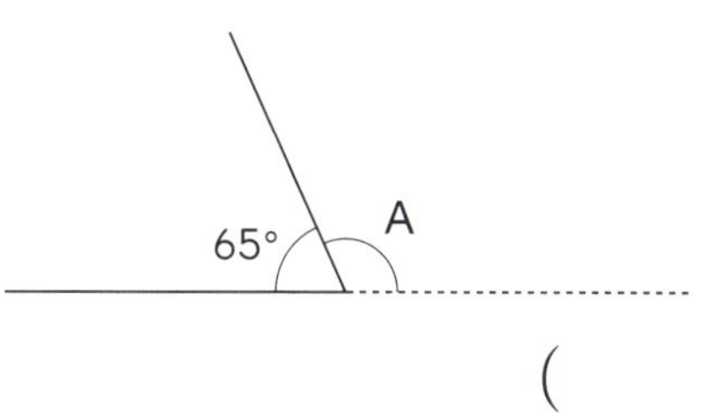

( )

(3)

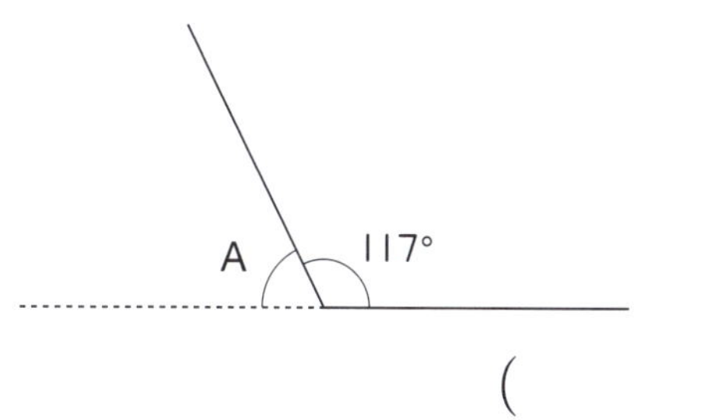

( )

2 Review the example. Then find angle A in each illustration below. 10 points per question

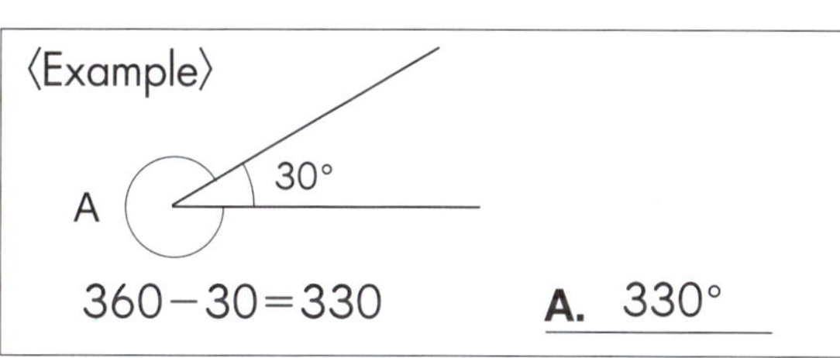

(1)

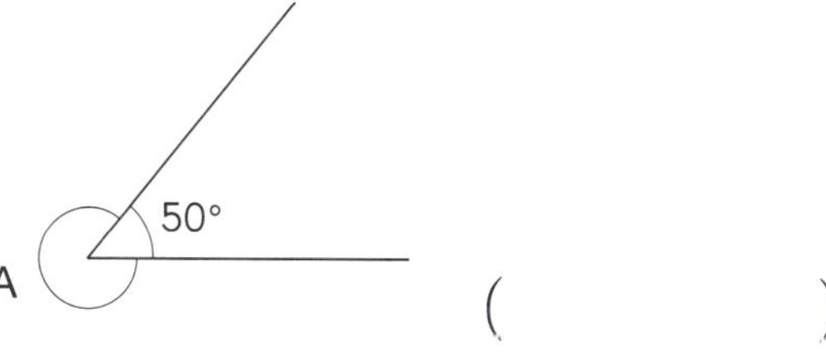

( )

(2)

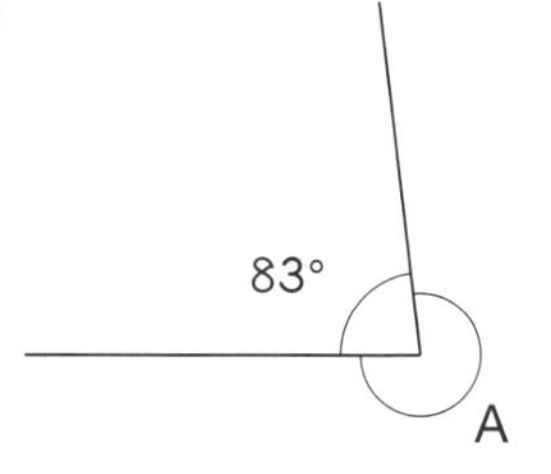

( )

(3)

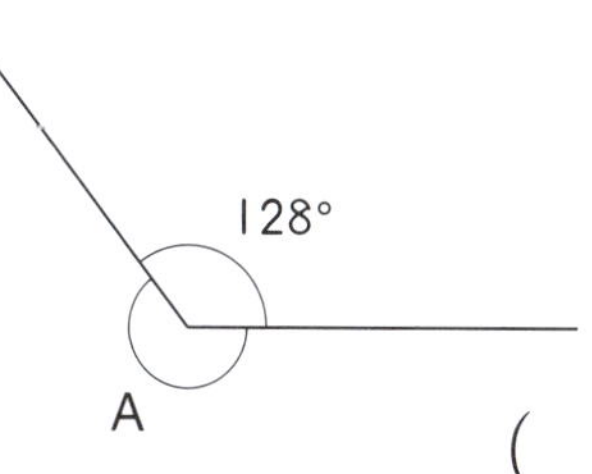

( )

3 Find angle A in each illustration below. 20 points per question

(1)

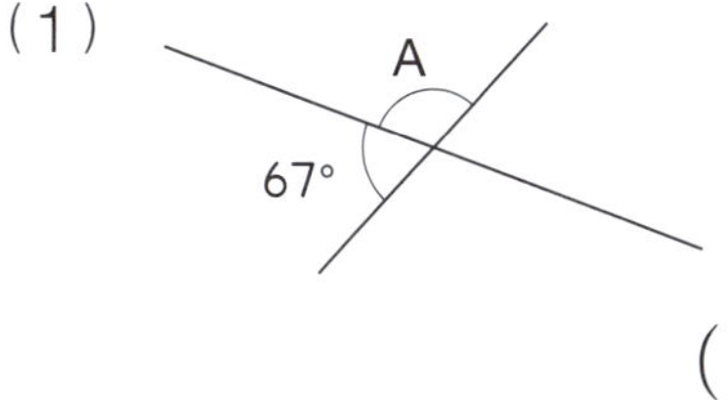

( )

(2)

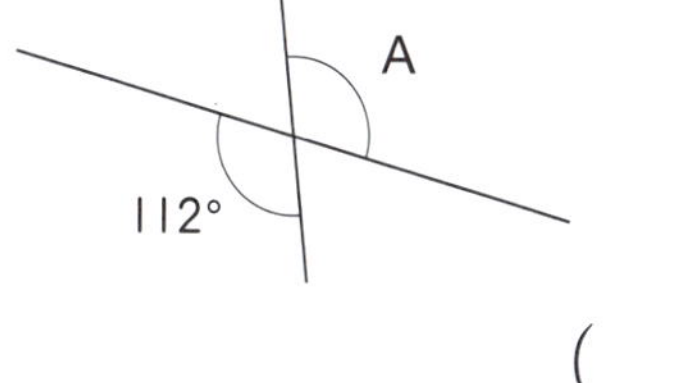

( )

Reading Comprehension

The Story of Doctor Dolittle 6

Date / / Name

Level ★★ Score /1

(1) Read the passage. Then answer the questions below. 20 points per quest

So that was the way the Doctor came to know that animals had a language of their own and could talk to one another. And all that afternoon, while it was raining, Polynesia sat on the kitchen table giving him bird words to put down in the book.

At tea-time, when the dog, Jip, came in, the parrot said to the Doctor, "See, he's talking to you."

"Looks to me as though he were scratching his ear," said the Doctor.

"But animals don't always speak with their mouths," said the parrot in a high voice, raising her eyebrows. "They talk with their ears, with their feet, with their tails—with everything. Sometimes they don't WANT to make a noise. Do you see now the way he's twitching up one side of his nose?"

"What's that mean?" asked the Doctor.

"That means, 'Can't you see that it has stopped raining?'" Polynesia answered. "He is asking you a question. Dogs nearly always use their noses for asking questions."

After a while, with the parrot's help, the Doctor got to learn the language of the animals so well that he could talk to them himself and understand everything they said. Then he gave up being a people's doctor altogether.

As soon as the Cat's-meat-Man had told every one that John Dolittle was going to become an animal-doctor, old ladies began to bring him their pet pugs and poodles who had eaten too much cake; and farmers came many miles to show him sick cows and sheep.

(1) What did Doctor Dolittle write down in his book?

The Doctor wrote down ____________________ in his book.

(2) Who was talking to Doctor Dolittle with his nose?

The ______________ was talking to the Doctor with his nose.

(3) How was the Doctor able to learn the language of the animals?

The Doctor was able to learn the language of the animals with the help of the

________________________.

(4) Why don't animals always speak with their mouths?

Animals don't always speak with their mouths because sometimes they don't want to make ______________.

(5) Who brought their sick animals to Doctor Dolittle?

The __________________ and the ________________ brought their sick animals.

1 Multiply or divide. 5 points per question

(1) 40×2	(5) 32×23	(9) $55\overline{)375}$	(13) $29\overline{)1506}$
(2) 273×3	(6) 115×134	(10) $8\overline{)5846}$	(14) $18\overline{)550}$
(3) 307×7	(7) 230×125	(11) $5\overline{)806}$	(15) $328\overline{)1810}$
(4) 201×113	(8) 16×7	(12) $123\overline{)222}$	(16) $97\overline{)732}$

2 Stamps are sold in rolls of 45. If Jane buys 12 rolls, how many stamps did she get? 10 points

Ans. ____________________

3 There are 196 roses, and the florist split them evenly into 14 bunches of roses. How many roses are in each bunch? 10 points

Ans. ____________________

Reading DAY 43

Review
The Moon Cake

Date / /

Name

Level ★★

Score /10

① Read the passage. Then answer the questions below.

A little monkey had a cake that a big monkey coveted. The big monkey made a plan to get the cake without making the little monkey cry so loud as to attract his mother's attention. The big monkey told the little monkey that the cake would be prettier if it were more like the moon. The big monkey thought that a cake like the moon must be beautiful, and on being assured by the big monkey that he had made many such moon cakes, he handed over his cake for manipulation. The big monkey took a big mouthful, leaving a crescent with jagged edges. The little monkey was not pleased by the change, and began to whimper; but the big monkey silenced him by saying that he would make the cake into a half-moon. So he nibbled off the horns of the crescent, and gnawed the edge smooth; but when the half-moon was made, the little monkey saw that there was hardly any cake left, and he again began to cry again. The big monkey again diverted him by telling him that, if he did not like so small a moon, he should have one that was just the size of the real thing. He then took the cake, and explained that, just before the new moon is seen, the old moon disappears. Then he swallowed the rest of the cake and ran away. And while little monkey waited for the new moon, the big monkey cried because his stomach hurt from too much cake.

(1) Choose words from the passage to complete the definitions below. 5 points per word

______________ **wanted to have something**

______________ **more attractive**

______________ **convinced; got rid of any doubts**

______________ **changes**

______________ **whine; cry; sob**

______________ **distracted; sidetracked**

(2) How did the big monkey trick the little monkey? 30 points for comp

The big monkey convinced the little monkey that the cake would be ______________ if it were more like the ______________.

(3) Complete the chart with words from the passage above. 40 points for com

Cause	Effect
The little monkey had a cake that the big monkey wanted.	The big monkey ______________ get the cake.
The big monkey took a big mouthful.	The little monkey began to ______________.
The big monkey ______________ the ______________ cake.	The big monkey's ______________ hurt.

Review

Level ★★

Date / /

Name

Score /100

Math DAY 44

1 Calculate. 5 points per question

(1) $\begin{array}{r} 1.7 \\ +\ 2.1 \\ \hline \end{array}$

(2) $\begin{array}{r} 2.1 \\ -\ 0.4 \\ \hline \end{array}$

(3) $\begin{array}{r} 12.5 \\ -\ 1.5 \\ \hline \end{array}$

(4) $\begin{array}{r} 3.7 \\ +\ 11.5 \\ \hline \end{array}$

(5) $\begin{array}{r} 0.5 \\ +\ 10.7 \\ \hline \end{array}$

(6) $\begin{array}{r} 12.5 \\ -\ 8 \\ \hline \end{array}$

(7) $\begin{array}{r} 1.07 \\ +\ 1.4 \\ \hline \end{array}$

(8) $\begin{array}{r} 2.3 \\ -\ 0.68 \\ \hline \end{array}$

2 Calculate. 5 points per question

(1) $\frac{3}{5} + \frac{1}{5} =$

(2) $\frac{2}{7} + \frac{3}{7} =$

(3) $\frac{4}{9} + \frac{3}{9} =$

(4) $\frac{4}{5} - \frac{1}{5} =$

(5) $\frac{6}{7} - \frac{3}{7} =$

(6) $\frac{7}{9} - \frac{5}{9} =$

3 Cindy's bag weighs 2.5 kilograms. Her sister's bag is 700 grams heavier. How much does her sister's bag weigh? Answer in kilograms. 15 points

Ans. ____________________

4 Fred's living room is 3 meters and 45 centimeters wide. His pictures are 40 centimeters wide, and he wants the pictures spaced equally as shown below. How much space should he put between the pictures in his living room? 15 points

Ans. ____________________

Review
William Shakespeare

Date / /

Name

Level ★★

Score /10

① Read the passage. Then answer the questions below. 100 points for co

William Shakespeare is an author who has been entertaining readers and theater audiences for centuries. His plays and poems appeared in the late 16th century in England and are still read and performed worldwide today.

It is unclear how Shakespeare's theater career began. Most of what we know about Shakespeare is from public records. It is known that Shakespeare arrived in London in his mid-twenties. He began modeling his own plays on the successful plays appearing in London theaters. Shakespeare had the most success with comedy—and particularly romantic comedies. Shakespeare also began including English history into his plays, which made his plays stand out. At that point in time, the historic play was a new genre (a category of art, such as in literature). Shakespeare blended comedy and tragedy to make the genre his own.

From 1594 and on he was a part of a theater group called "Lord Chamberlain's Men." This group became a big hit at the Globe Theatre in London. The Globe Theatre had a unique design—the building was a circular shape and the audience would gather around the stage in a semi-circle. Shakespeare staged many of his plays specifically for the Globe Theatre.

Around 1594, Shakespeare also began writing *Romeo and Juliet*, which would become one of his most famous plays. The play focuses on a young man and woman who fall in love but are torn apart because their families are enemies. *Romeo and Juliet* continues to be performed and adapted for stage, film, television and more. Indeed, Shakespeare's plays are as alive today as they were in 16th century England.

(1) Who was William Shakespeare?

William Shakespeare was an __________.

(2) What did Shakespeare write?

Shakespeare wrote __________ and __________.

(3) Where did Shakespeare stage many of his plays?

Shakespeare staged many of his plays at the ________________ in __________.

(4) When did Shakespeare begin working with Lord Chamberlain's Men?

Shakespeare began working with Lord Chamberlain's Men in ________.

(5) How did Shakespeare stage his plays?

Shakespeare staged many of his plays specifically for the ________________.

(6) Why did Shakespeare's plays about English history stand out?

Shakespeare's plays about English history stood out because they were a new __________, and he blended __________ and __________.

Review

Level ★★

Date / /

Name

Score /100

Math DAY 45

1 How much time has passed from the time on the left to the time on the right? 15 points per question

(1)

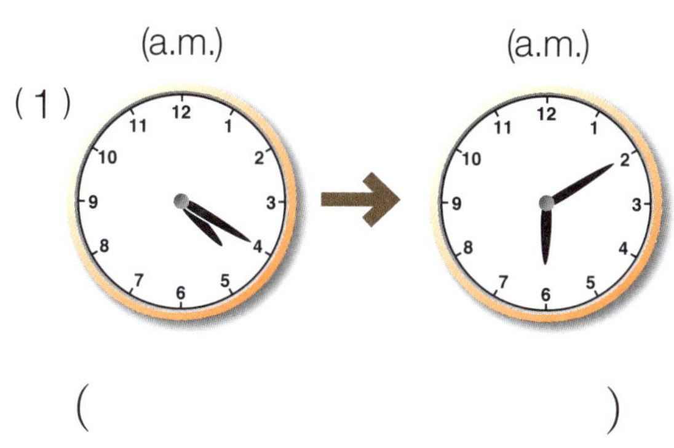

( )

(2)

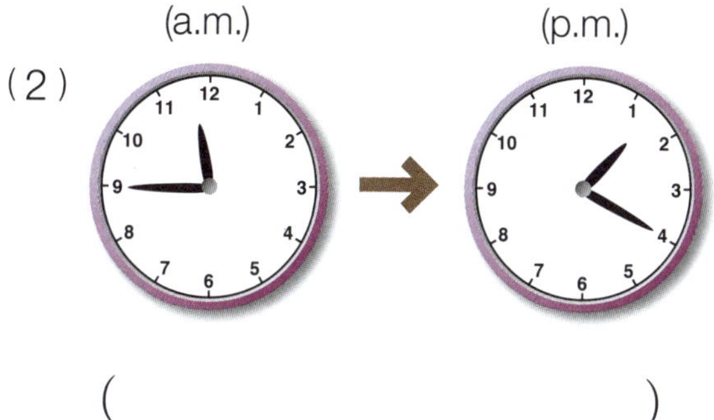

( )

2 As pictured on the right, you have a sphere that fits snugly inside a box.  10 points per question

(1) How long is each side of the box?  ( )

(2) How long is the diameter of the sphere? ( )

(3) How long is the radius of the sphere?  ( )

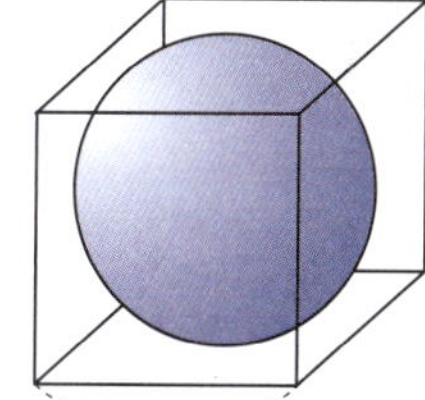

3 Find angle A in each illustration below.  10 points per question

(1)

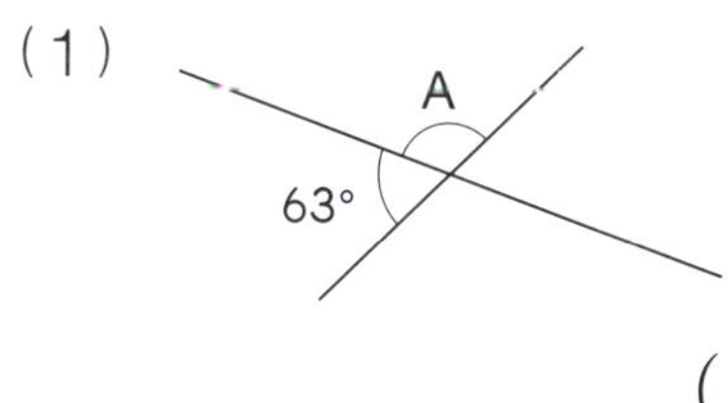

( )

(2)

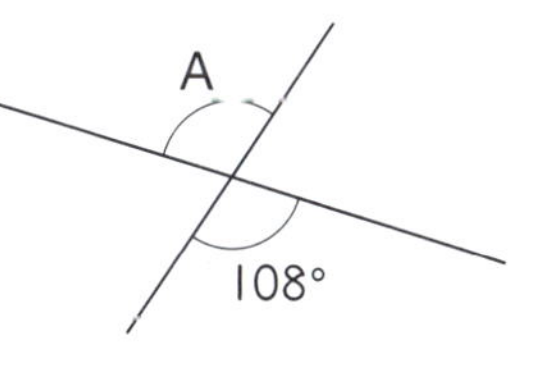

( )

4 Calculate the volume of the following rectangular, solid shapes—also called prisms. Answer in cubic inches.  10 points per question

(1)

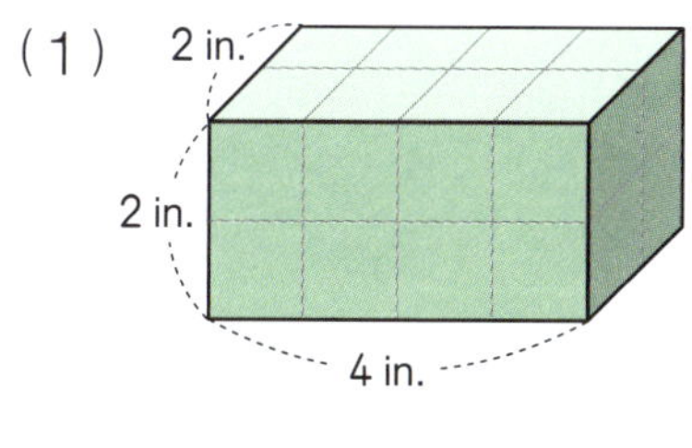

( )

(2) 2 in. 3 in. 5 in.

( )

Reading DAY 45

Review
Around and Around

Date / /　Name

Level ★★　Score /10

① Read the passage. Then answer the questions below. 25 points per question

Have you ever seen a professional cyclist ride upside-down in a loop? The cyclist is taking advantage of different forces at work: centrifugal force and centripetal force.

The same force is at work if a person swings a bucket of water. By attaching a small bucket of water to the end of a rope, a person can swing the bucket in a circle fast enough so that the water will not spill out. The water tends to stay in a straight line and so it pushes toward the bottom of the bucket. This is called centrifugal force—the tendency for any object to continue to move in a straight line and move away from the center. Centripetal force also is working at the same time. Centripetal force is the force that keeps an object moving along a curved path, so the force is directed inward toward the center. The rope is the centripetal force that keeps the bucket moving in a circle. Without the rope (or if you let go of the rope), the bucket would immediately fly off in a straight line.

Both centrifugal and centripetal force help the professional cyclist perform his trick. As the cyclist travels up the loop and upside-down at the top, he stays on the track because of centrifugal force. The cyclist and the bike continue to move in a straight line. Meanwhile, the track acts as the centripetal force that keeps the cyclist moving in a circular direction.

(1) Describe the way the bucket and the bike must be moving in order to do the trick.

The bucket and the bike must be moving ______________ in order to do the trick.

(2) What can the professional cyclist do because of centrifugal and centripetal force?

The professional cyclist can ride ______________ in a loop.

(3) What is the main idea of the whole passage?

The main idea is that a cyclist takes advantage of ______________ force and ______________ force to ride upside-down in a loop.

(4) What details support the main idea? Put a check (✓) next to the answers.

( ) The cyclist and the bike continue to move in a straight line.
( ) The force of gravity holds objects down.
( ) The track keeps the cyclist moving in a circular direction.
( ) Many inventions use centrifugal and centripetal force.

Wow! You finished! Congratulations!

DAY 1, pages 1 & 2

❶ Multiply.

(1) 13 × 2 = 26 (2) 34 × 2 = 68 (3) 23 × 3 = 69 (4) 43 × 3 = 129 (5) 32 × 4 = 128
(6) 43 × 4 = 172 (7) 24 × 5 = 120 (8) 37 × 5 = 185 (9) 27 × 6 = 162 (10) 48 × 6 = 288
(11) 31 × 7 = 217 (12) 53 × 7 = 371 (13) 25 × 8 = 200 (14) 39 × 8 = 312 (15) 16 × 9 = 144
(16) 57 × 9 = 513 (17) 60 × 4 = 240 (18) 73 × 2 = 146 (19) 36 × 3 = 108 (20) 84 × 5 = 420

① Read each word aloud. Then divide the word into syllables.

(1) airplane air/plane
(2) parachute par/a/chute
(3) scrapbook scrap/book
(4) automobile au/to/mo/bile
(5) highway high/way
(6) computer com/put/er
(7) basketball bas/ket/ball
(8) spectators spec/ta/tors

② Write the words with the same amount of syllables in each group below.

alligator propeller hollow overboard pelican motorcycle dictionary badger hurdle

(a) 2 syllables: badger, hollow, hurdle
(b) 3 syllables: overboard, pelican, propeller
(c) 4 syllables: alligator, dictionary, motorcycle

DAY 2, pages 3 & 4

❶ Multiply.

(1) 130 × 4 = 520 (2) 273 × 2 = 546 (3) 408 × 3 = 1224 (4) 318 × 3 = 954 (5) 116 × 4 = 464
(6) 347 × 4 = 1388 (7) 227 × 5 = 1135 (8) 547 × 5 = 2735 (9) 409 × 6 = 2454 (10) 647 × 6 = 3882
(11) 503 × 7 = 3521 (12) 381 × 7 = 2667 (13) 308 × 8 = 2464 (14) 459 × 8 = 3672 (15) 207 × 9 = 1863
(16) 728 × 9 = 6552 (17) 274 × 6 = 1644 (18) 686 × 7 = 4802 (19) 778 × 8 = 6224 (20) 889 × 9 = 8001

① Complete the table below according to the example.

adjective	adverb	adjective	adverb
immediate	immediately	lazy	lazily
deliberate	deliberately	sleepy	sleepily
normal	normally	merry	merrily
polite	politely	helpful	helpfully
rapid	rapidly	generous	generously
playful	playfully	light	lightly
swift	swiftly	dainty	daintily

② Read the passage. Then answer the questions below using only adverbs from the passage.

An old woman with a large bag boarded a bus that rapidly drove away. Immediately, a young man generously gave his seat to her. Normally, most people would swiftly take the seat and politely thank the man for being so helpful. Instead, the woman daintily laid her bag on the seat and remained standing. Was the woman deliberately being rude? No, she merrily explained that inside the bag was a litter of sleepy kittens. She was carefully taking them to a new home.

(1) How did the bus drive? The bus drove rapidly.
(2) When did the young man give up his seat? The young man gave up his seat generously.
(3) How would people normally react to the young man's offer? Normally, most people would politely thank the man.
(4) How did the woman lay her bag down? The woman laid her bag down daintily.
(5) How was the woman taking the kittens to a new home? The woman was carefully taking the kittens to a new home.

DAY 3, pages 5 & 6

❶ Multiply.

(1) 32 × 12 = 64, 32, 384 (2) 42 × 23 = 126, 84, 966 (3) 43 × 34 = 172, 129, 1462 (4) 54 × 37 = 378, 162, 1998 (5) 34 × 45 = 170, 136, 1530
(6) 46 × 42 = 92, 184, 1932 (7) 23 × 52 = 46, 115, 1196 (8) 38 × 55 = 190, 190, 2090 (9) 47 × 60 = 2820 (10) 28 × 61 = 28, 168, 1708
(11) 32 × 74 = 128, 224, 2368 (12) 53 × 72 = 106, 371, 3816 (13) 29 × 81 = 29, 232, 2349 (14) 34 × 83 = 102, 272, 2822 (15) 26 × 93 = 78, 234, 2418
(16) 54 × 91 = 54, 486, 4914 (17) 50 × 41 = 50, 200, 2050 (18) 67 × 24 = 268, 134, 1608 (19) 35 × 38 = 280, 105, 1330 (20) 84 × 58 = 672, 420, 4872

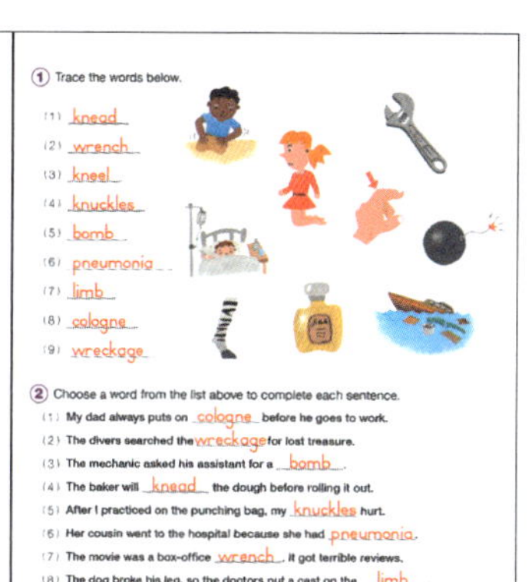
① Trace the words below.

(1) knead (2) wrench (3) kneel (4) knuckles (5) bomb (6) pneumonia (7) limb (8) cologne (9) wreckage

② Choose a word from the list above to complete each sentence.

(1) My dad always puts on cologne before he goes to work.
(2) The divers searched the wreckage for lost treasure.
(3) The mechanic asked his assistant for a bomb.
(4) The baker will knead the dough before rolling it out.
(5) After I practiced on the punching bag, my knuckles hurt.
(6) Her cousin went to the hospital because she had pneumonia.
(7) The movie was a box-office wrench, it got terrible reviews.
(8) The dog broke his leg, so the doctors put a cast on the limb.
(9) When we finally got to the cave, we had to kneel because the ceiling was so low.

DAY 4, pages 7 & 8

❶ Multiply.

(1) 322 × 13 = 966, 322, 4186 (2) 322 × 33 = 966, 966, 10626 (3) 314 × 14 = 1256, 314, 4396 (4) 314 × 45 = 1570, 1256, 14130 (5) 407 × 24 = 1628, 814, 9768
(6) 423 × 51 = 423, 2115, 21573 (7) 906 × 37 = 6342, 2718, 33522 (8) 316 × 70 = 22120 (9) 609 × 55 = 3045, 3045, 33495 (10) 370 × 38 = 2960, 1110, 14060
(11) 135 × 16 = 810, 135, 2160 (12) 534 × 47 = 3738, 2136, 25098 (13) 412 × 67 = 2884, 2472, 27604 (14) 619 × 58 = 4952, 3095, 35902 (15) 270 × 50 = 13500
(16) 164 × 56 = 984, 820, 9184 (17) 672 × 32 = 1344, 2016, 21504 (18) 608 × 89 = 5472, 4864, 54112 (19) 731 × 44 = 2924, 2924, 32164 (20) 345 × 95 = 1725, 3105, 32775

① Complete the passage using vocabulary words defined below.

The sloth is an animal that lives up to its name, which means "laziness." These (1) mammals are (2) infamous for being slow and sleeping up to twenty hours a day. Sloths (3) dwell in the trees of the tropical forests in Central and South America. While their (4) lengthy arms and wooly fur make them look like monkeys, they are more closely related to armadillos and anteaters. There are two main (5) species of sloth. Sloths with two toes hang upside-down, while sloths with three toes like to sit upright. Three-toed sloths also have an extra (6) vertebrae in their necks so they can turn their heads almost all the way around. Both types of sloth are slow. In fact, they're so slow that (7) algae grows on their fur. Some scientists think that sloth moves slow so (8) predators won't see them. The green algae also acts as (9) camouflage. But they're not only slow moving—a sloth can take up to a month to (10) digest one meal.

infamous have a bad reputation
vertebrae a section of bone or cartilage that make up the spinal column
dwell to stay for a while; to live in a place
algae any plant or plantlike living creature similar to seaweed
species a category of living things; a class of things of the same kind and with the same name
digest to break down food and absorb it in the body
predators animals that lives by killing and eating other animals
camouflage the hiding or disguising of something by covering it up or changing the way it looks
mammals warm-blooded animals with vertebrae that feed their babies with window.
lengthy very long

DAY 5, pages 9 & 10

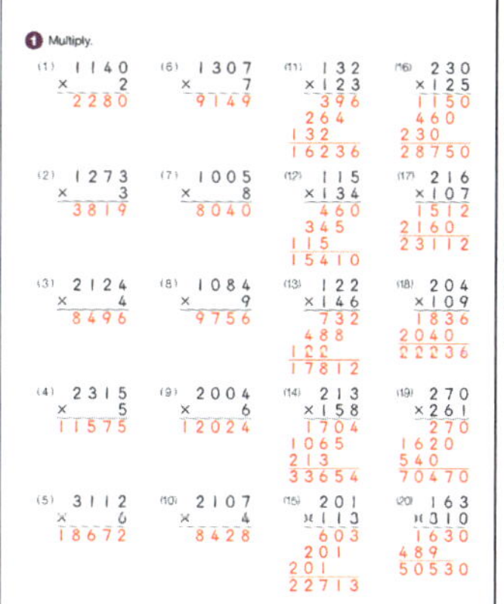
❶ Multiply.

(1) 1140 × 2 = 2280 (2) 1273 × 3 = 3819 (3) 2124 × 4 = 8496 (4) 2315 × 5 = 11575 (5) 3112 × 6 = 18672
(6) 1307 × 7 = 9149 (7) 1005 × 8 = 8040 (8) 1084 × 9 = 9756 (9) 2004 × 6 = 12024 (10) 2107 × 4 = 8428
(11) 132 × 123 = 396, 264, 132, 16236 (12) 115 × 134 = 460, 345, 115, 15410 (13) 122 × 146 = 732, 488, 122, 17812 (14) 213 × 158 = 1704, 1065, 213, 33654 (15) 201 × 113 = 603, 201, 201, 22713
(16) 230 × 125 = 1150, 460, 230, 28750 (17) 216 × 107 = 1512, 2160, 23112 (18) 204 × 109 = 1836, 2040, 22236 (19) 270 × 261 = 270, 1620, 540, 70470 (20) 163 × 310 = 1630, 489, 50530

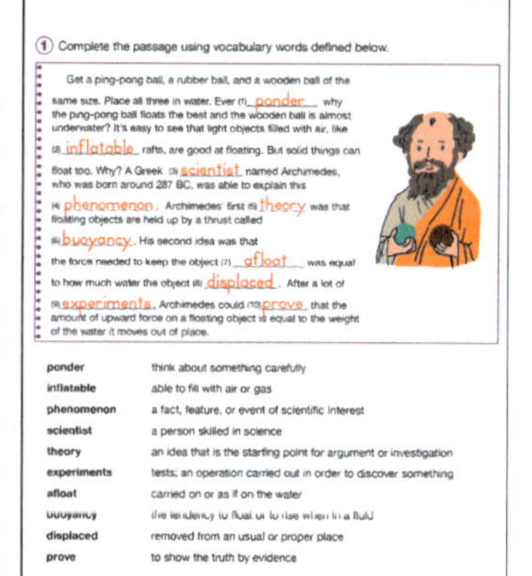
① Complete the passage using vocabulary words defined below.

Get a ping-pong ball, a rubber ball, and a wooden ball of the same size. Place all three in water. Ever (1) ponder why the ping-pong ball floats the best and the wooden ball is almost underwater? It's easy to see that light objects filled with air, like (2) inflatable rafts, are good at floating. But solid things can float too. Why? A Greek (3) scientist named Archimedes, who was born around 287 BC, was able to explain this (4) phenomenon. Archimedes' first (5) theory was that floating objects are held up by a thrust called (6) buoyancy. His second idea was that the force needed to keep the object (7) afloat was equal to how much water the object (8) displaced. After a lot of (9) experiments, Archimedes could (10) prove that the amount of upward force on a floating object is equal to the weight of the water it moves out of place.

ponder think about something carefully
inflatable able to fill with air or gas
phenomenon a fact, feature, or event of scientific interest
scientist a person skilled in science
theory an idea that is the starting point for argument or investigation
experiments tests; an operation carried out in order to discover something
afloat carried on or as if on the water
buoyancy the tendency to float or to rise when in a fluid
displaced removed from an usual or proper place
prove to show the truth by evidence

DAY 6, pages 11 & 12

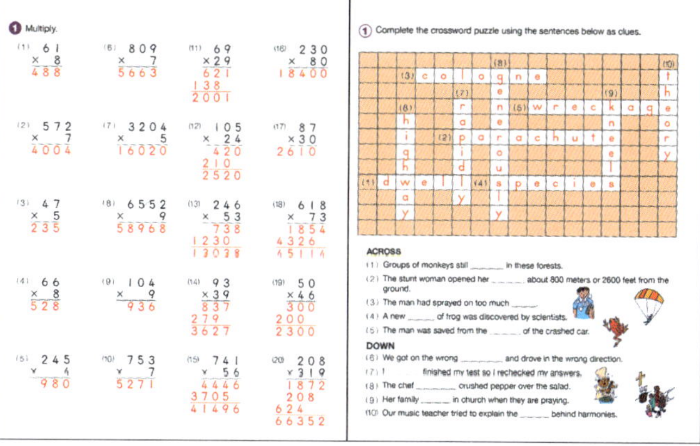
❶ Multiply.

(1) 61 × 8 = 488 (2) 572 × 7 = 4004 (3) 47 × 5 = 235 (4) 66 × 8 = 528 (5) 245 × 4 = 980
(6) 809 × 7 = 5663 (7) 3204 × 5 = 16020 (8) 6552 × 9 = 58968 (9) 104 × 9 = 936 (10) 753 × 7 = 5271
(11) 69 × 29 = 621, 138, 2001 (12) 105 × 24 = 420, 210, 2520 (13) 246 × 53 = 738, 1230, 13038 (14) 93 × 39 = 837, 279, 3627 (15) 741 × 56 = 4446, 3705, 41496
(16) 230 × 80 = 18400 (17) 87 × 30 = 2610 (18) 618 × 73 = 1854, 4326, 45114 (19) 50 × 46 = 300, 200, 2300 (20) 208 × 319 = 1872, 208, 624, 66352

① Complete the crossword puzzle using the sentences below as clues.

Across: (1) dwell (2) parachute (3) cologne (4) species (5) wreckage
Down: (6) highway (7) rapidly (8) generously (9) kneel (10) theory

ACROSS
(1) Groups of monkeys still ______ in these forests.
(2) The stunt woman opened her ______ about 800 meters or 2600 feet from the ground.
(3) The man had sprayed on too much ______.
(4) A new ______ of frog was discovered by scientists.
(5) The man was saved from the ______ of the crashed car.

DOWN
(6) We got on the wrong ______ and drove in the wrong direction.
(7) I ______ finished my test so I rechecked my answers.
(8) The chef ______ crushed pepper over the salad.
(9) Her family ______ in church when they are praying.
(10) Our music teacher tried to explain the ______ behind harmonies.

DAY 7, pages 13 & 14

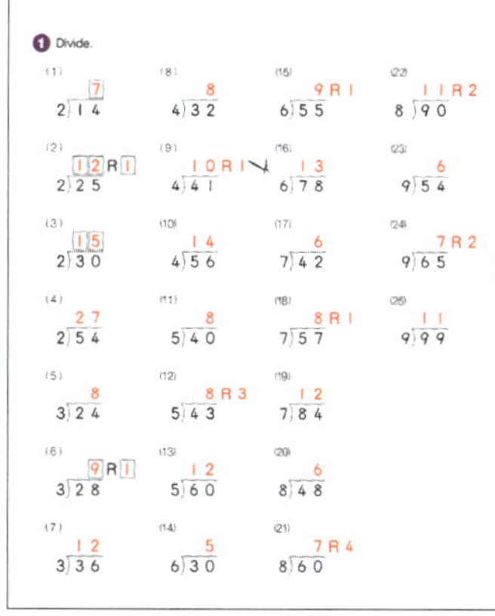
❶ Divide.

(1) 14 ÷ 2 = 7 (2) 25 ÷ 2 = 12 R 1 (3) 30 ÷ 2 = 15 (4) 54 ÷ 2 = 27 (5) 24 ÷ 3 = 8 (6) 28 ÷ 3 = 9 R 1 (7) 36 ÷ 3 = 12
(8) 32 ÷ 4 = 8 (9) 41 ÷ 4 = 10 R 1 (10) 56 ÷ 4 = 14 (11) 40 ÷ 5 = 8 (12) 43 ÷ 5 = 8 R 3 (13) 60 ÷ 5 = 12 (14) 30 ÷ 6 = 5
(15) 55 ÷ 6 = 9 R 1 (16) 78 ÷ 6 = 13 (17) 42 ÷ 7 = 6 (18) 57 ÷ 7 = 8 R 1 (19) 84 ÷ 7 = 12 (20) 48 ÷ 8 = 6 (21) 60 ÷ 8 = 7 R 4
(22) 90 ÷ 8 = 11 R 2 (23) 54 ÷ 9 = 6 (24) 65 ÷ 9 = 7 R 2 (25) 99 ÷ 9 = 11

① Read the short passage. Then choose words from the passage to complete the definitions below.

Canada is the second largest country in the world, but it only has half of one percent of the world's **population**. That means a lot of open space. Canada has lakes, rivers, mountains, **plains**, forests, and swamps. It even has the only **temperate** rain forest in the world. Canada **spans** more than half of the Northern **Hemisphere**. In the far north of Canada, you can see ice, snow, and **glaciers**.

With all this space comes many different animals—bears, mountain lions, otters and many freshwater fish. Canadians **cherish** nature and wildlife. Forty-one national parks and three marine **conservation** areas have been made to protect animals like the wolf and **lynx**. These animals need to be protected because they have been **overhunted**.

(1) glaciers large bodies of ice that move slowly
(2) cherish to hold dear; to keep with care and affection
(3) conservation a careful protection of something
(4) plains broad areas of level or rolling treeless country
(5) lynx a large wild cat
(6) population the whole number of people living in a country or region
(7) overhunted hunted too much
(8) temperate a climate that is usually mild without very cold or hot temperatures
(9) spans reaches or extends across
(10) hemisphere half of the earth

DAY 8, pages 15 & 16

❶ Divide.

(1) 224 ÷ 2 = 112 (2) 208 ÷ 2 = 104 (3) 150 ÷ 2 = 75 (4) 150 ÷ 3 = 50 (5) 315 ÷ 3 = 105 (6) 320 ÷ 3 = 106 R 2 (7) 140 ÷ 4 = 35
(8) 408 ÷ 4 = 102 (9) 350 ÷ 4 = 87 R 2 (10) 350 ÷ 5 = 70 (11) 570 ÷ 5 = 114 (12) 473 ÷ 5 = 94 R 3 (13) 630 ÷ 6 = 105 (14) 450 ÷ 6 = 75
(15) 726 ÷ 6 = 121 (16) 455 ÷ 7 = 65 (17) 721 ÷ 7 = 103 (18) 500 ÷ 7 = 71 R 3 (19) 840 ÷ 8 = 105 (20) 454 ÷ 8 = 56 R 6 (21) 616 ÷ 8 = 77
(22) 198 ÷ 9 = 22 (23) 354 ÷ 9 = 39 R 3 (24) 505 ÷ 9 = 56 R 1 (25) 963 ÷ 9 = 107

① Read the short passage. Then choose words from the passage to complete the definitions below.

A long time ago people learned something that would **alter** history: people learned how to **harness** fire. By striking stones together, a person could make a **spark**. Most likely, two **minerals** were used as **equipment** for starting fires. They gave off sparks when hit with something hard. The other **method** of creating fire was rubbing wooden sticks together. Just as your hands get warm when you rub them together, the **friction** of wood being rubbed together **generates** heat. **Tinder** would be put nearby to catch fire.

When a fire is lit, it creates light. The flame's color can tell you how hot the flame is and how much energy is being **released**. A bright blue flame is very hot and a dull yellow flame is cooler.

(1) method a way, plan, or procedure for doing something
(2) spark a bright flash; a small bit of burning material
(3) equipment tools; necessary items used for a purpose
(4) minerals natural materials usually from the ground
(5) generates causes; brings into existence
(6) harness to put to work; use
(7) tinder a material that burns easily
(8) released set free
(9) friction the rubbing of one thing against another
(10) alter change; to make different in some particular

DAY 9, pages 17 & 18

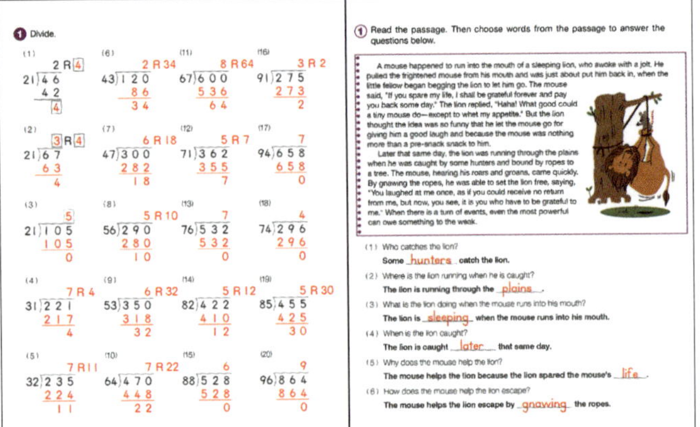

DAY 10, pages 19 & 20

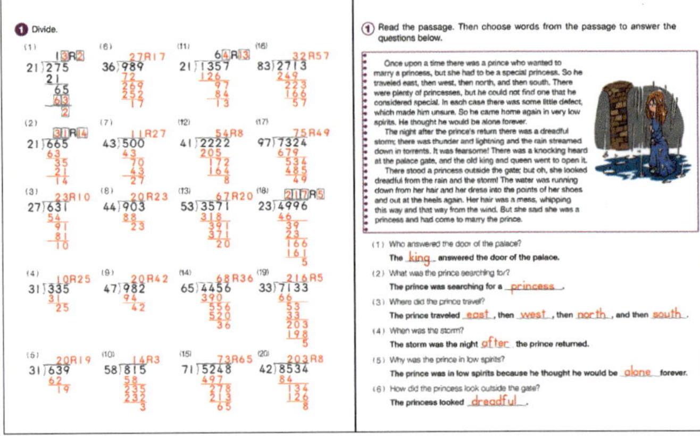

DAY 11, pages 21 & 22

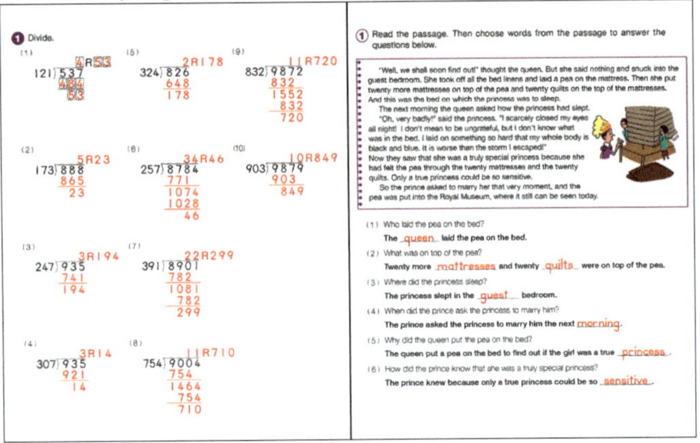

DAY 12, pages 23 & 24

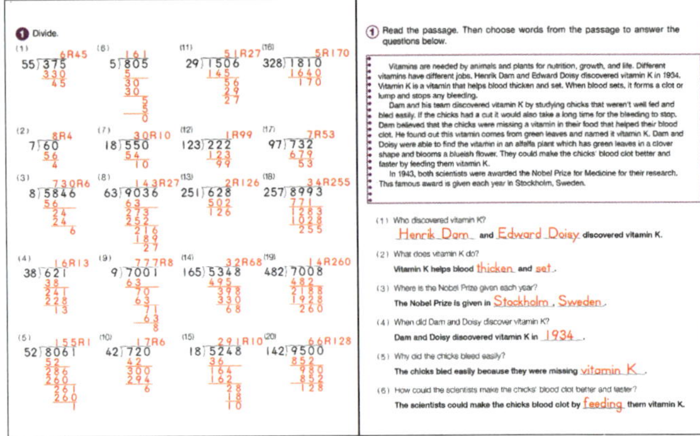

DAY 13, pages 25 & 26

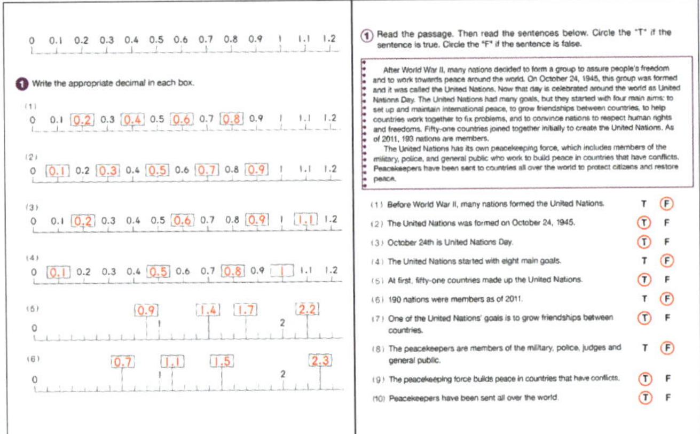

DAY 14, pages 27 & 28

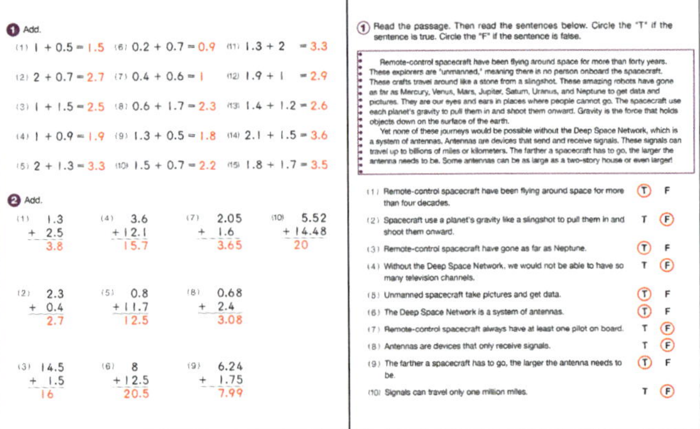

DAY 15, pages 29 & 30

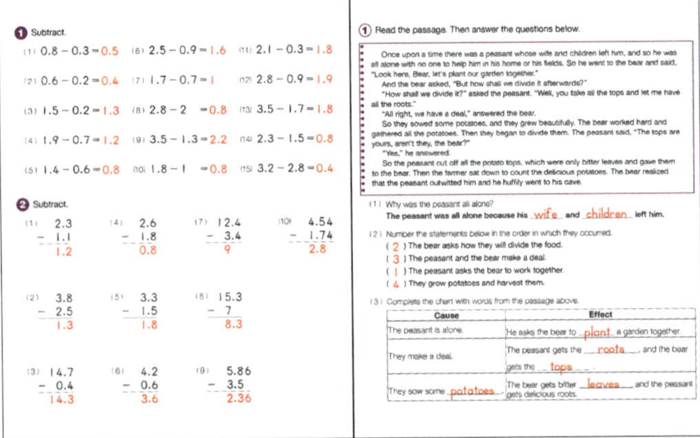

DAY 16, pages 31 & 32

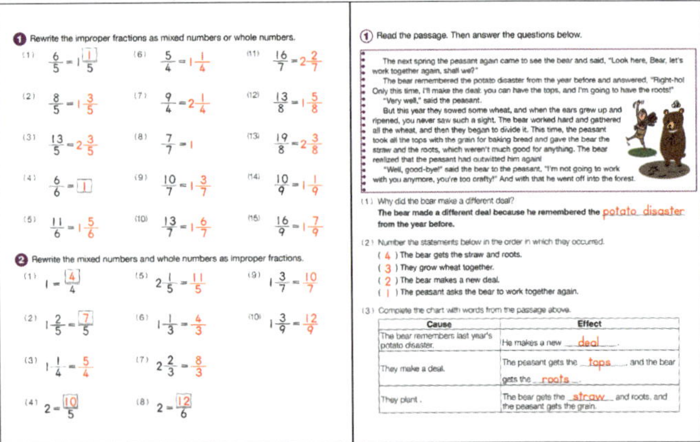

DAY 17, pages 33 & 34

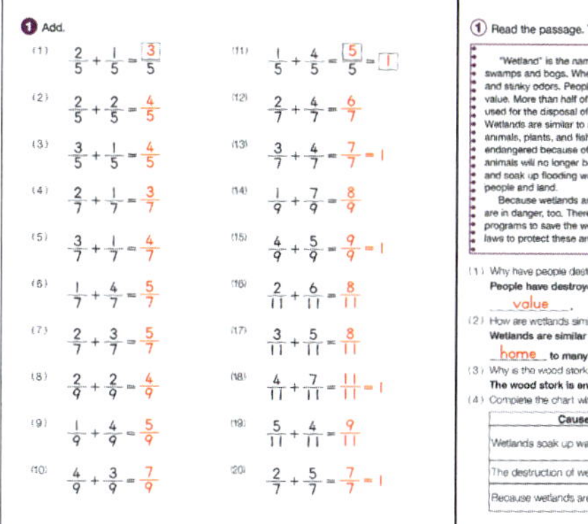

DAY 18, pages 35 & 36

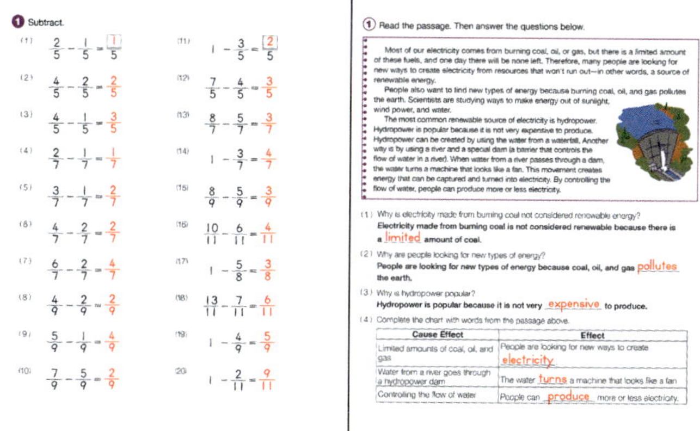

DAY 19, pages 37 & 38

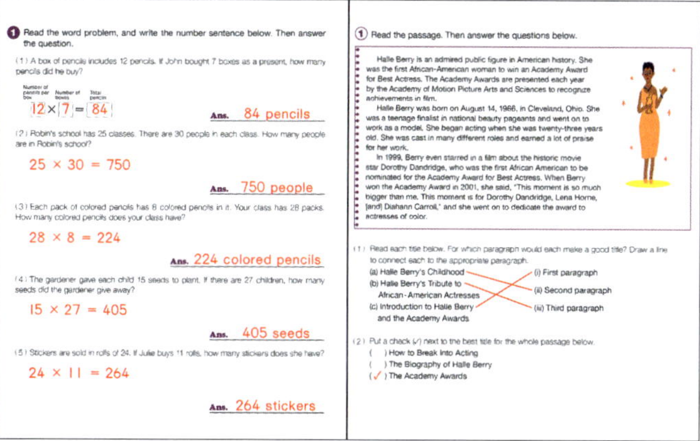

DAY 20, pages 39 & 40

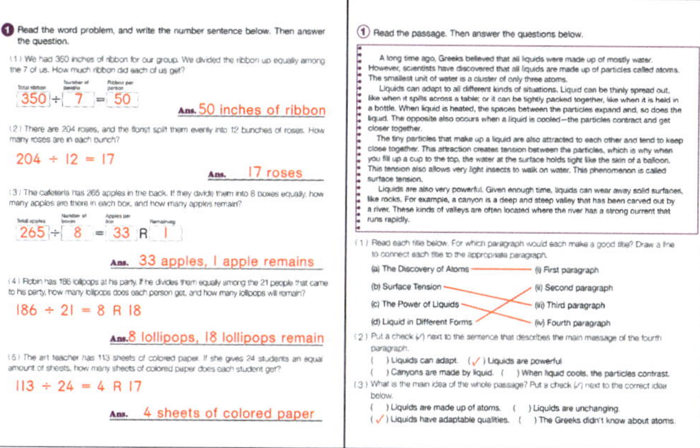

DAY 21, pages 41 & 42

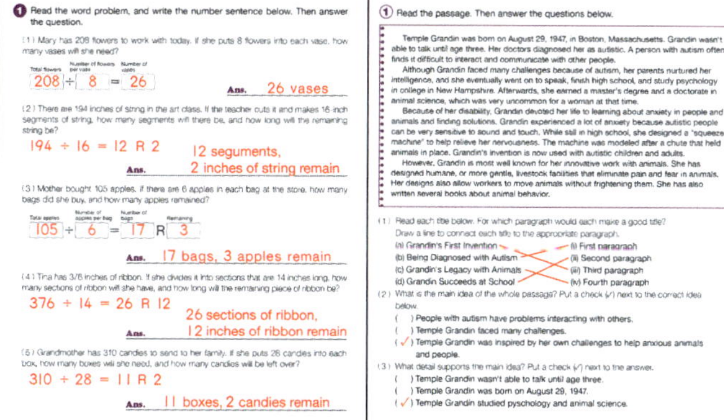

DAY 22, pages 43 & 44

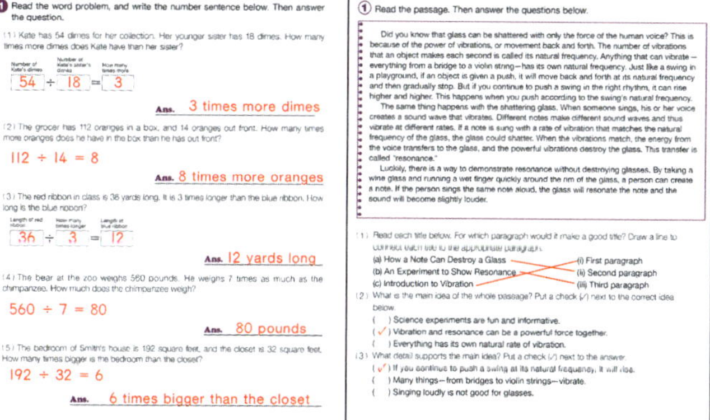

DAY 23, pages 45 & 46

1 Read the word problem, and write the number sentence below. Then answer the question.

(1) You used 0.2 pounds of sugar in your cake, and 1.7 pounds of sugar are left over. How much sugar was there in the beginning?

$0.2 + 1.7 = 1.9$

Ans. 1.9 pounds of sugar

(2) Julian's bag weighs 2.8 pounds, and his father's bag is 1.2 pounds heavier than his. How much does his father's bag weigh?

$2.8 + 1.2 = 4$

Ans. 4 pounds

(3) Dan and Wendy were trying to throw a big rock. Dan threw it 1.3 meters. Wendy threw it 70 centimeters further. How far did Wendy throw the rock?

70 cm = 0.7 m

$1.3 + 0.7 = 2$

Ans. 2 meters

(4) Ava's bag weighs 2.4 kilograms. Her sister's bag is 600 grams heavier. How much does her sister's bag weigh?

600 g = 0.6 kg

$2.4 + 0.6 = 3$

Ans. 3 kilograms

(5) Kelly had 2.1 liters of water in her water bottle. Her big water bottle can hold 800 milliliters more. How much can her big water bottle hold?

$2.1 + 0.8 = 2.9$

Ans. 2.9 liters

① Read the passage. Then answer the questions below.

Roberto Clemente was one of the first Latin American baseball stars. He was born in a modest house in Puerto Rico on August 18, 1934. Clemente went on to become a twelve-time All Star and do important charity work in his free time.

At only fourteen years old, Clemente began playing softball on a men's team. By eighteen, he turned professional. In February of 1954, the Brooklyn Dodgers recruited Clemente but placed him in the minor leagues, where he didn't play very often. The Dodgers tried to hide his talent so other teams wouldn't want him. But it was too late—the Pittsburgh Pirates brought Clemente up to the major leagues.

Over eighteen seasons, Clemente collected impressive statistics and delighted baseball fans. No matter what kind of pitch, he could hit the ball. He had lightning speed, which made him a great base runner. He was also well known for his powerful and accurate throwing arm. Even towards the end of his career, Clemente continued to set records.

But one of the biggest challenges Clemente faced was racial prejudice. Many baseball fans, reporters, and players were rude or nasty to Clemente because he was black and Latino. However, he always defended his rights and the rights of others. Clemente said, "My greatest satisfaction comes from helping to erase the old opinion about Latin Americans and blacks."

On December 31, 1972, Clemente died in a plane crash only a few miles from where he was born. He was on his way to deliver aid to earthquake victims in Nicaragua. He was only thirty-eight, but he had become a baseball legend.

(1) Complete the main ideas for each paragraph in the chart below.

Paragraph	Main idea
First paragraph	Introduction to Roberto Clemente.
Second paragraph	The start of Clemente's baseball career.
Third paragraph	Clemente set baseball records and delighted fans.
Fourth paragraph	Clemente faced racial prejudice.
Fifth paragraph	Clemente died young but had become a baseball legend.

(2) What is the main idea of the whole passage? Put a check (✓) next to the correct idea below.

( ) Over eighteen seasons, Clemente set impressive records.
( ) Clemente helped many people and fought racial prejudice.
(✓) Clemente overcame many challenges, became a baseball legend and helped people.

DAY 24, pages 47 & 48

1 Read the word problem, and write the number sentence below. Then answer the question.

(1) Selena wrapped all the presents for her friends this year. If she used 1.6 yards of ribbon out of the 2.3 yards of ribbon she had, how much ribbon is left?

$2.3 - 1.6 = 0.7$

Ans. 0.7 yard of ribbon

(2) We had 3 pounds of flour before my mother cooked me a birthday cake and used 0.3 pound of flour. How much flour do we have now?

$3 - 0.3 = 2.7$

Ans. 2.7 pounds of flour

(3) We have 2.4 liters of orange juice in the fridge. We also have apple juice, but 500 milliliters less. How much apple juice do we have in the fridge?

500 mL = 0.5 L

$2.4 - 0.5 = 1.9$

Ans. 1.9 liters of apple juice

(4) Brad and Mark both have wizard staffs. Brad's is 2.1 meters long. If Brad's staff is 50 centimeters longer than Mark's, how long is Mark's wizard staff?

$2.1 - 0.5 = 1.6$

Ans. 1.6 meters

(5) My bag of pears is 0.8 kilograms heavier than your bag of pineapples. If my bag of pears weighs 2 kilograms, how much does your bag of pineapples weigh?

$2 - 0.8 = 1.2$

Ans. 1.2 kilograms

① Read the excerpt from *The Tale of Mr. Tod* by Beatrix Potter. Then answer the questions below using words from the passage.

I have made many books about well-behaved people. Now, for a change, I am going to make a story about two disagreeable people, called Tommy Brock and Mr. Tod. Nobody could call Mr. Tod "nice." The rabbits could not bear him; they could smell him half a mile off. He was of a wandering habit and he had foxey whiskers; they never knew where he would be next.

One day he was living in a stick-house in the coppice, causing terror to the family of old Mr. Benjamin Bouncer. Next day he moved into a pollard willow near the lake, frightening the wild ducks and the water rats.

In winter and early spring he might generally be found in an earth amongst the rocks at the top of Bull Banks, under Oatmeal Crag.

He had half a dozen houses, but he was seldom at home.

The houses were not always empty when Mr. Tod moved out; because sometimes Tommy Brock moved in; (without asking leave).

Tommy Brock was a short, bristly, fat, waddling person with a grin; he grinned all over his face. He was not nice in his habits. He ate wasp nests and frogs and worms; and he waddled about by moonlight, digging things up.

His clothes were very dirty; and as he slept in the daytime, he always went to bed in his boots.

(1) What type of characters will the author write a story about?

The author will write about two disagreeable **people.**

(2) Put a check (✓) next to the words that describe Mr. Tod.

( ) nice ( ) unmoving (✓) smelly
(✓) wanderer (✓) never home ( ) musical
( ) animal-friendly (✓) unpredictable ( ) funny

(3) Put a check (✓) next to the words that describe Tommy Brock.

(✓) smily ( ) tall (✓) short
( ) nice (✓) dirty ( ) talented
( ) normal (✓) strange ( ) smart

(4) Despite it being daytime, what did Tommy Brock do?

Tommy Brock slept **in the daytime.**

DAY 25, pages 49 & 50

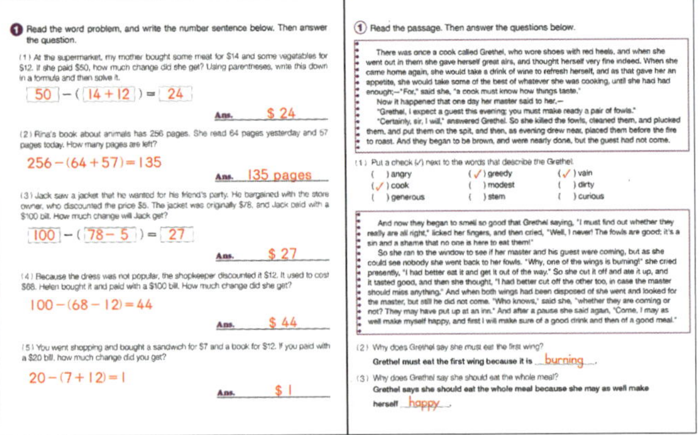

DAY 26, pages 51 & 52

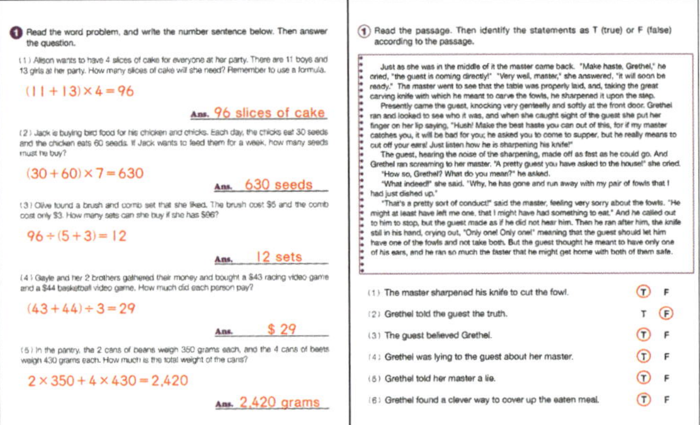

DAY 27, pages 53 & 54

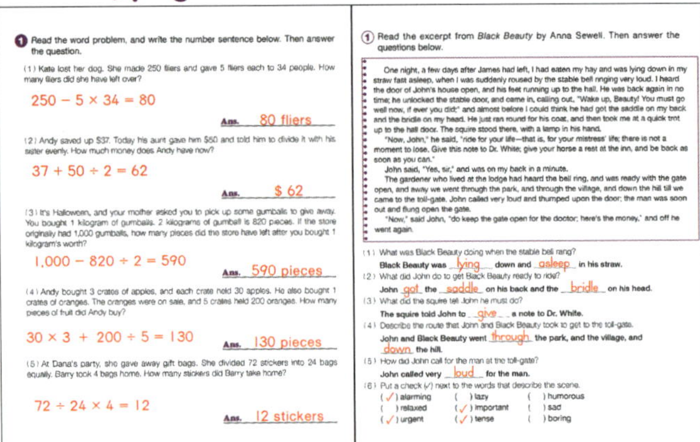

DAY 28, pages 55 & 56

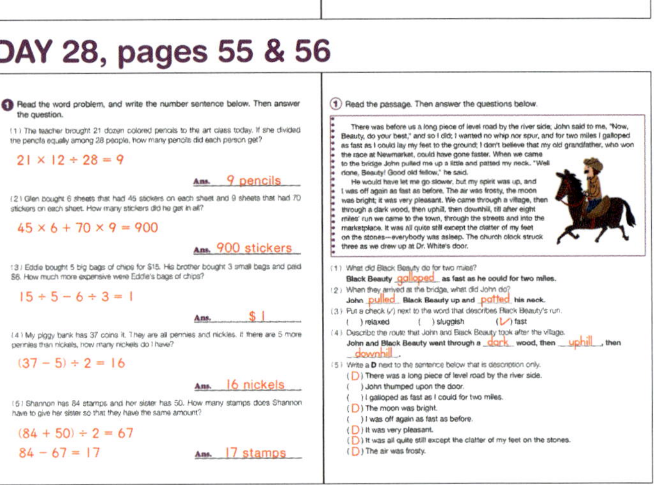

DAY 29, pages 57 & 58

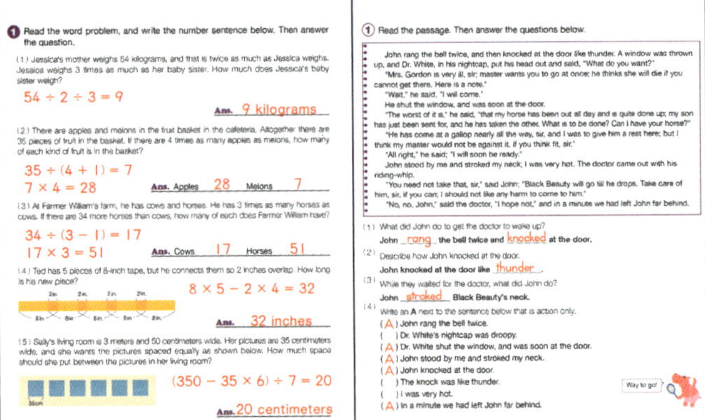

DAY 30, pages 59 & 60

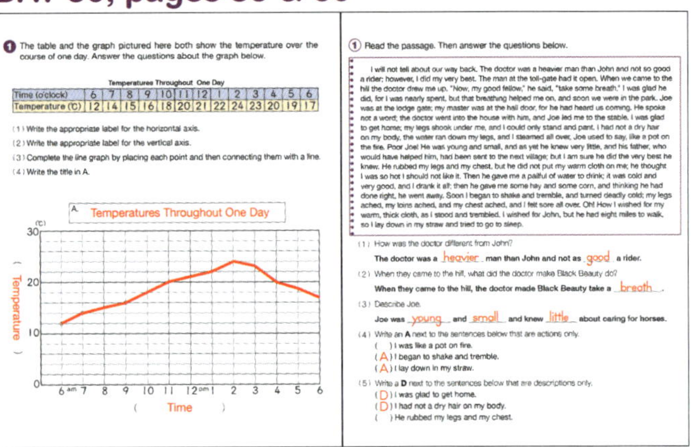

DAY 31, pages 61 & 62

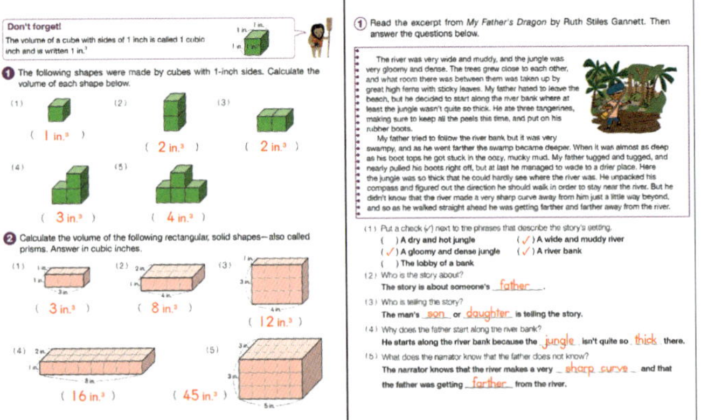

DAY 32, pages 63 & 64

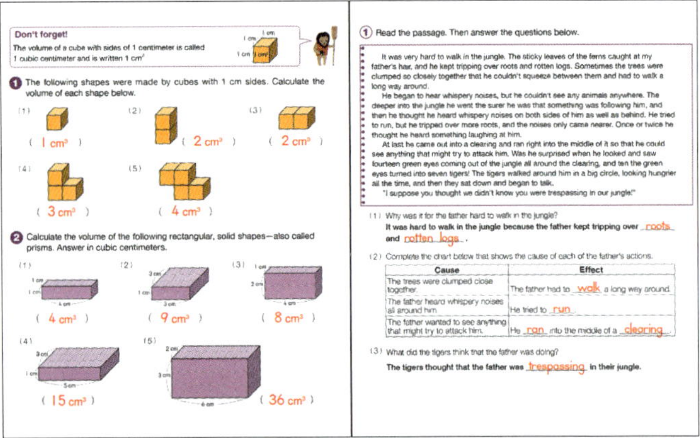

DAY 33, pages 65 & 66

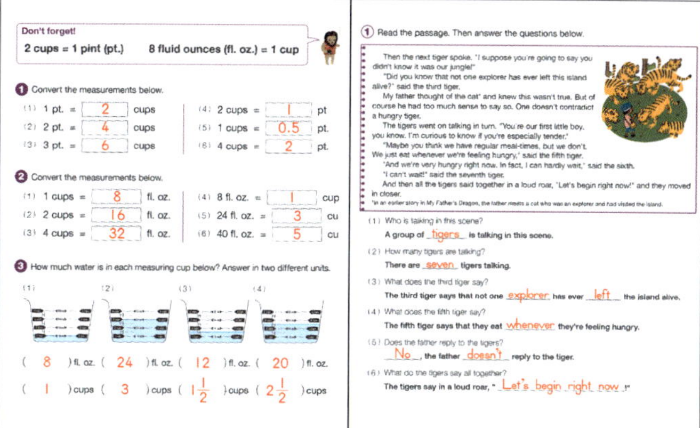

DAY 34, pages 67 & 68

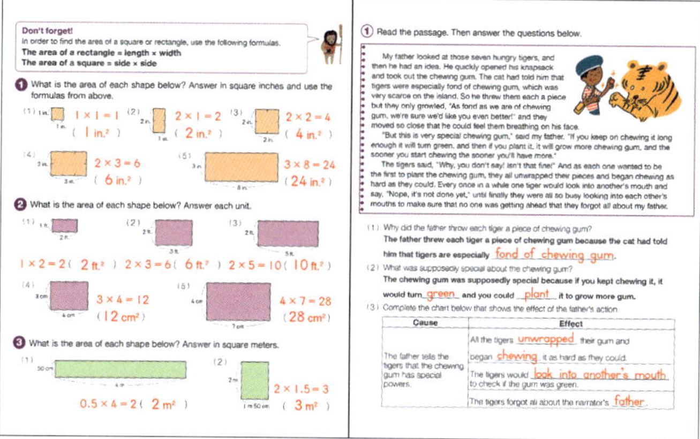

DAY 35, pages 69 & 70

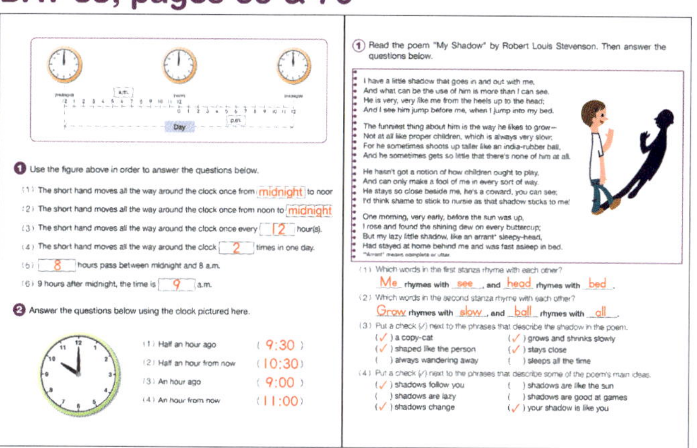

DAY 36, pages 71 & 72

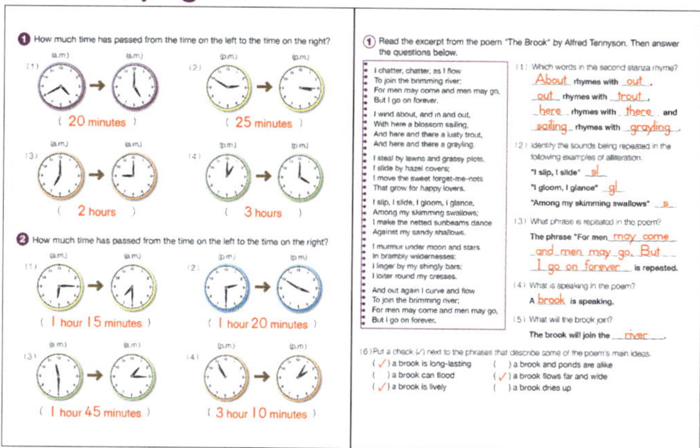

DAY 37, pages 73 & 74

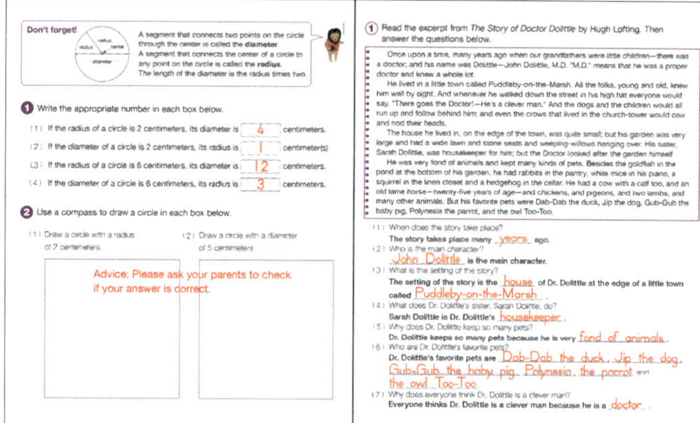

DAY 38, pages 75 & 76

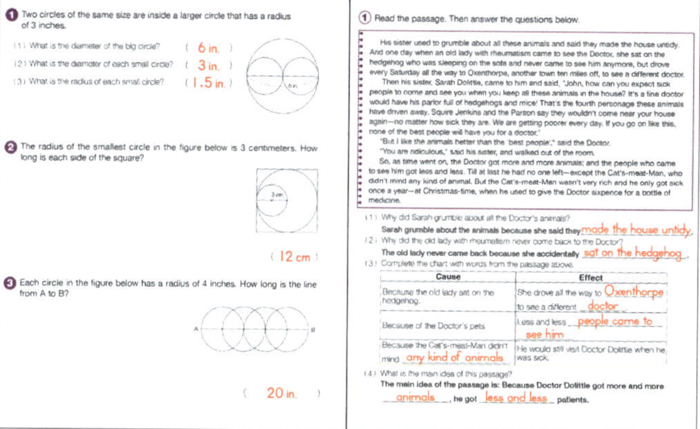

DAY 39, pages 77 & 78

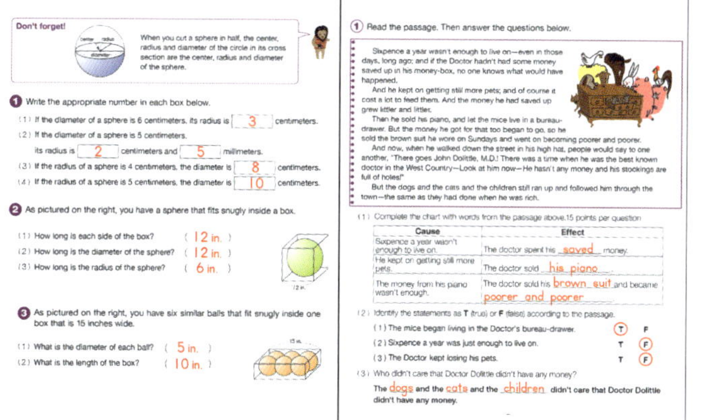

DAY 40, pages 79 & 80

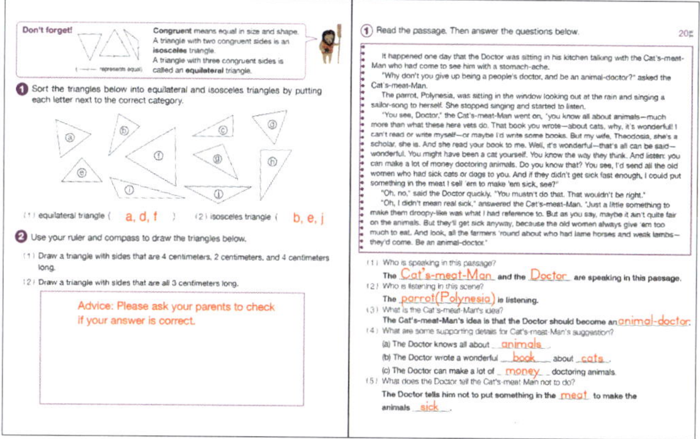

DAY 41, pages 81 & 82

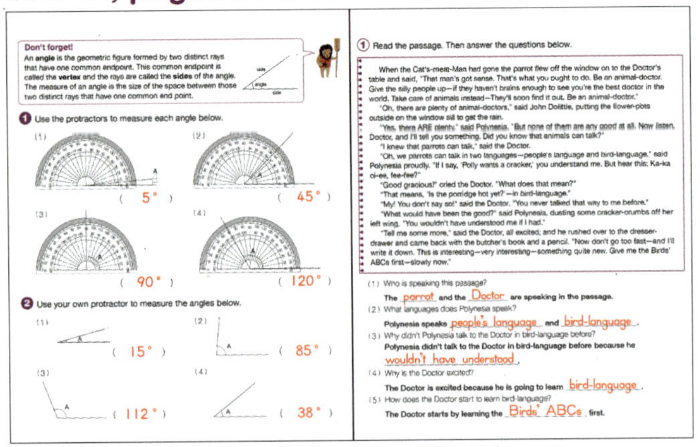

DAY 42, pages 83 & 84

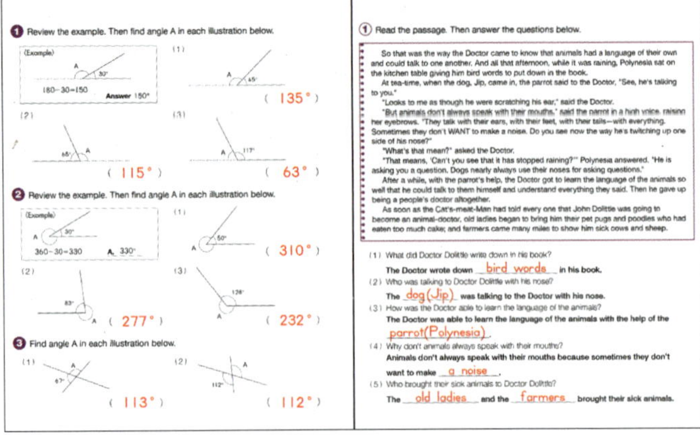

DAY 43, pages 85 & 86

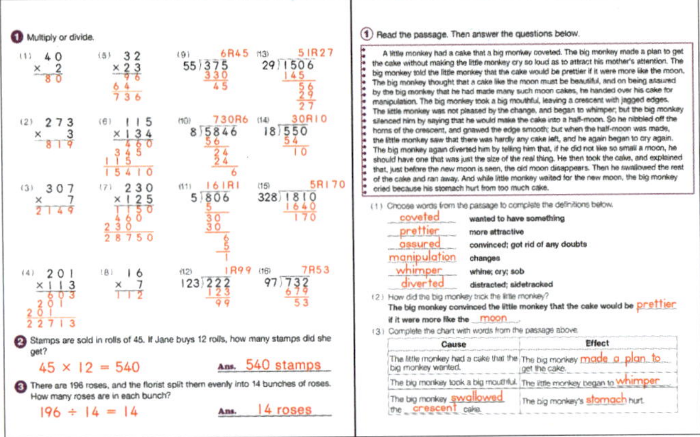

DAY 44, pages 87 & 88

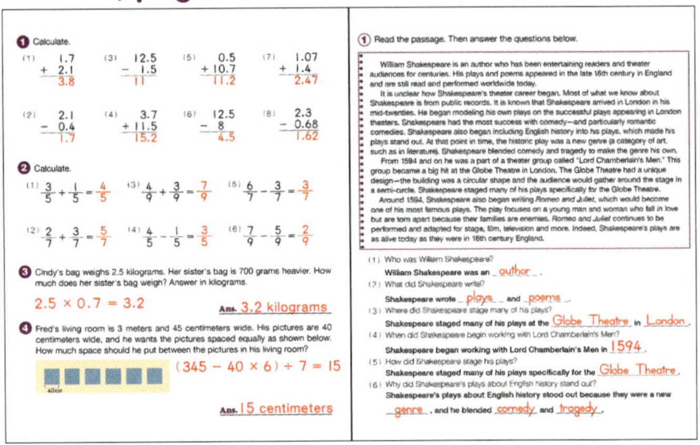

DAY 45, pages 89 & 90

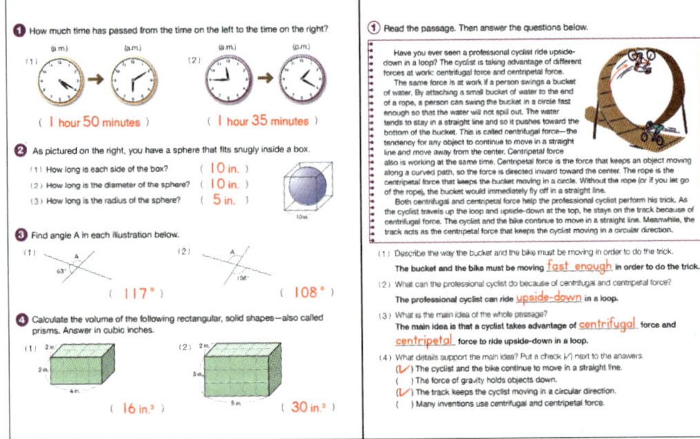